THE AGILE
THINKER

THE AGILE THINKER

BETTER WAYS OF LIVING, WORKING, AND MAKING SENSE OF LIFE'S CHAOS

JACK WALSER

NEW DEGREE PRESS

COPYRIGHT © 2020 JACK WALSER

THE AGILE THINKER

Better Ways of Living, Working, and Making Sense of Life's Chaos

ISBN   978-1-63676-110-7 *Paperback*
         978-1-63676-111-4 *Kindle Ebook*
         978-1-63676-112-1 *Ebook*

The Agile Thinker isn't a book; it's a new way of thinking about work, about life, and about how we interact with the chaos that life throws at us. Read it. Join us. Move ever forward.

"Go back?" he thought. "No good at all!
Go sideways? Impossible! Go forward?
Only thing to do! On we go!"

—J.R.R. TOLKIEN, *THE HOBBIT, OR*
THERE AND BACK AGAIN

"Damn the torpedoes! Jouett, full speed!
Four bells, Captain Drayton!"

—ADMIRAL DAVID GLASGOW FARRAGUT, DURING
THE BATTLE OF MOBILE BAY, AUGUST 5, 1864

CONTENTS

———

INTRODUCTION TO THE INTRODUCTION   11

SECTION ONE.   **THE MOVEMENT**   **21**

CHAPTER 1.   THE SCIENCE BEHIND THE AGILE THINKER 25

CHAPTER 2.   MAKING LIFE EASIER BY MASTERING
YOUR WIP   39

SECTION TWO.   **THE FOUNDATIONS**   **57**

CHAPTER 3.   MAKING THE LEAP: BECOMING AN
AGILE THINKER   59

CHAPTER 4.   GETTING ALIGNED   69

CHAPTER 5.   WHAT'S YOUR STORY?   75

CHAPTER 6.   MASTERING SPACE AND TIME USING
BACKLOGS   87

CHAPTER 7.   OUR NEW NORMAL: MANAGING
BACKLOGS AMIDST A PANDEMIC, AND
OTHER CHEERFUL TOPICS   93

CHAPTER 8.   CONNECTING THE DOTS: MANAGING
YOUR FLOW AS AN AGILE THINKER   101

SECTION THREE. THE STORIES   **113**

CHAPTER 9.   LAWYERS CAN BE AGILISTS TOO!   115

CHAPTER 10.   HERDING CATS: USING AGILE TO
                APPLY TO COLLEGE   125

CHAPTER 11.   WHY AND HOW I WROTE THIS BOOK
                AS AN AGILE THINKER   135

                ACKNOWLEDGEMENTS   139

                APPENDIX   141

INTRODUCTION TO THE INTRODUCTION

———

"There is opportunity in chaos."

A consultant once said this to me while we were engaged in a large, strategically significant transformational program. The implication was that the more chaos we could encounter in delivering the initiative, the more money we could make by extending the problem.

I was horrified. While I love opportunity, I am not a super huge fan of creating opportunity at the expense of a client. I do believe in chaos, though, especially in the learnings that people like you and me can take from it.

Before I dive into that, though, a bit about me: my name is Jack and I am a former management consultant, now serving in a leadership position in the healthcare industry. I love what I do and am enjoying this chapter of my life, especially since my career has been a wild series of twists and turns that produced a personal resume reflecting a totally non-traditional path to get to where I am now. A dear friend once described my resume as "unique, to the point of being obscure," but I prefer to refer to it as "never a dull moment."

College was the last point at which I felt my life was "traditional." I went through four years, paid for by your tax dollars (thank you, by the way), and afterward started my adult life as an officer in the United States Navy. Four years, two ships, thirty-nine countries, and two foreign wars later, I left to begin consulting. I worked with a large, Big Four firm before transitioning to a group that built combat systems for the Navy and foreign governments. My main client was a foreign navy, which took me all over. The travel and experiences were amazing. A few years into that job, I got the entrepreneurial itch and started my own firm, one that focused on process excellence for clients inside and outside the federal government sector. From there, I went on to co-manage a presidential campaign in Sub-Saharan Africa and co-found a large school security initiative in Texas.

You know... as you do.

This was chaos—good chaos—but I was starting to have a crisis around my purpose, as my experiences weren't the resume-building approach that many of my peers took to get to where they were at the time. I reflected on what I had done to date and realized that I had a common thread throughout every initiative I took part in, from the days I spent in the military right up to the present: transformation. I had a passion for transforming people, processes, and technology, and regardless of the project or the medium it was where I was the happiest.

I took that passion and created my motto, "ever forward." In essence, that motto is my attempt to let everyone know that I do not believe in process for process' sake, despite my multiple decades now serving as a process or transformational leader. No, I am different: In my younger, wilder days I was the type of leader that understood the construct, but in a devil-may-care fashion that let the rank and file know I was all about getting "stuff" done while not being down with the drudgery of process. My professional certifications got me in the door, but my right-brained approach to delivery won the hearts and minds of the general population. Driven by some professional ability and a high level of self-assurance— after all, I was the guy who was never picked last in kickball (most dingers, 1985), or in team selection for transformation projects—I believed I was a true asset to any organization that would welcome my expertise[1].

In reality, I was just another young person making his way through his early thirties, trying to get to that seemingly insurmountable destination called "retirement." I took pride in the fact that my professional acumen helped some of the world's largest companies (and several of its smallest) become more efficient and effective in their operations. I wore those achievements around like a badge of honor, until the ultimate efficiency system killer introduced itself into my life.

Children.

---

1   *See, e.g.,* legend status for most dingers, St. Henry School, 1985.

Kids are amazing. Those who choose to have them know what I'm talking about here: innocent smiles, the pitter patter of little feet, etc. I have four of them, three boys and a girl, whom I love deeply. They are amazing creatures, all. My kids do their level best to challenge, stimulate, frustrate, enrage, and introduce just enough chaos—both constructive and negative—to make any professional certification in efficiency or process improvement utterly useless. I should be good at it, as I spent several years of my professional life learning how to optimize systems and make operations run more smoothly. For example, I got a master's degree in systems engineering/engineering management only to realize that running a household with six people in it is something that I was unqualified to do in any capacity. My seemingly insurmountable "ever forward" motto gradually shifted to "mostly forward," and then to "any port in a storm." I needed a new system, one that was different from what I had been taught, as that clearly was not working.

Enter Agile—a concept that, once learned, quickly changed the way that I looked at my life, my job, and, ultimately, the way I helped run my family.

I first came in contact with the Agile methodology in early 2008 and was instantly hooked. It was a relatively new practice at that time, a brief seven years into its existence. As I read about it and studied how it came about, I realized that it was less of a framework or methodology and more of a movement. At its core, Agile was a way by which a community of software developers changed the world. The cohort, which was largely made up of a group of professionals who were tired of developing software using a dated technique designed for 1960s-era defense projects, focused on getting products to market faster. Their goal was to develop a new way of working that focused less on process and more on getting things done with real transparency, predictability, and quality. There were few rules in the design. Instead, their approach was based on a manifesto (but the non-violent, non-government watch list type of manifesto) and had four main components that made Agile less of a movement for software developers and more of a movement for the rest of us:

- It focused on individuals and interactions, not processes and tools;
- It advocated for a focus on a (software) product that works and not exit criteria stemming from a bunch of obsolete documentation;
- It pushed its adopters to collaborate, not negotiate what has to fit in between the traditional project start and project end dates; and
- It allowed for teams to pivot based on changes versus following a linear plan.

I was hooked. This, to me, seemed like a very human response to tried-and-true practices that have made up the core of product development, and it appealed directly to my right-brained views on delivery and time management. I was 100 percent in and decided to invest all of my time, energy, and, in some cases, money to educate myself on this amazing movement. What Agile represented to me at the time was a way to manage my personal and professional life. Consider the following:

1. According to British psychologist Dr. Richard Wiseman, the overall pace of life has increased by 10-30 percent since the mid-1990s.[2]

2. For most of us born before 1980, the mid-1990s seem as if they ended approximately thirty minutes ago, lending credence to Dr. Wiseman's hypothesis.

3. For all of us born after 1900 (which, hopefully, should be all of us), speed isn't always a positive thing. While great on a broadband connection, it is generally dangerous on highways and ski slopes. It tends to wreak havoc for me whenever life's great mysteries are hurtling themselves in the form of four short(er) people.

So, I did what any normal consultant would do: I got certified via a two-day class, took a test, and thankfully passed. My training class was taught by not just a regular, run-of-the mill instructor, but an actual signer of that manifesto—one of those pioneers whose voice rang from the proverbial desert and drove change. I was now a bona fide, certified, and justified Agile expert. I even took my education one step further and began to dive more deeply into learning about how to take Agile principles and apply them at scale—because even the largest organizations with the most complex IT products need to be on this bus too.

And I was successful. Sure, I failed along the way, but I learned from those failures and turned them into rock-solid,

---

2   Christine Louise Hohlbaum, "How Can We Keep Up in This Fast-Paced World?" *The Power of Slow* (blog), *Psychology Today*, November 14, 2009.

no-I-swear-I-will-never-do-those-again, scarred but smarter learnings that would guide my approach to working with my clients. Starting small, I worked my way to larger and larger projects that became programs (called something different in Agile parlance). The programs eventually scaled to large organizational Agile "transformations" that instantly became my favorite type of client engagement. Hands down.

A "transformation" is typically a large initiative that a company undertakes when it wants to completely change the way it does something. As you can probably imagine, the lift is heavy: in order to complete a transformation successfully, you need an expert (namely, *moi*) who is able to define the change, educate the workforce on how to implement the change, and ensure that the employees adopt the new way of working. It's a lot.

Agile transformations became my favorite primarily because I could be the expert in the eyes of the C-suite. I could be the person who took their companies from operating in an old, outdated way to the new world of organizational efficiency and productivity. Using Agile I could educate entire workforces on how their organizations could move from Waterfall delivery, with all of its processes and artifacts, to something new and better.

I got pretty good at it too. Before I knew it, I implemented this methodology on a small level at one of the world's largest mobile handset manufacturers, at scale at a large insurance company, at one of the nation's largest manufacturers of building materials (you've heard of it; if not, it's most likely the organization that is holding the walls of your house up), and at a law firm.

A law firm? Building materials?

After some reflection (read: seven minutes), I realized that only one of those organizations actually *really* focused on technology and the effective and efficient delivery of code. The common thread, though, was a single, unified desire to take large groups of overworked employees and make them more effective, efficient, and engaged. After all, I was told, an effective, efficient, and engaged employee is an effective, efficient, but retained employee, which is apparently a big deal.

This reflection drove further reflection. If any of us can be successful implementing this methodology in areas that don't traditionally need it, is there a practical application in our daily lives? Could a working parent benefit from focusing on interaction over processes and tools (like a Dr. Spock manual? Not sure.)? My hypothesis and "ever forward," winning attitude said "yes." Besides, I realized I had a gap in managing my family life that I was sure other people had too.

In this book, I try to look at the world in the same way those signers of the Agile manifesto looked at the status quo of software delivery and project management: with a keen eye toward improving the process, making things easier to do, and keeping themselves and others sane in the process. This is the singular focus of this book and is now becoming a personal philosophy of mine.

Section One presents a high-level view of how I got here, so I present an overview of Agile to educate the reader on the basis of the movement. If you know Agile and are a certified, bona fide expert, then skip it. Just be well aware that you're going to miss out on the author viewpoints and several dad jokes. Your call. If you're not familiar with Agile, these chapters will serve as a general guide to get you grounded in Agile theory and fact. While they won't make you an expert, they will provide direction and context that will allow you to adopt some of the recommendations and principles that I posit will make your lives easier!

Section Two begins to lay out the foundation for your Agile existence: a practical, pragmatic, real-life approach that you can take in your daily life to make it easier, make you more productive, or just make you look like a genius at cocktail parties. The beautiful part of all this (the movement, the cottage industry surrounding the movement, and the tangible results companies large and small are reaping from the movement) is that it takes very little experience to apply and is not constrained by industry or educational field. It applies to all professions and walks of life, so much so that clergy, tradespeople, and professionals alike, regardless of industry, will benefit.

Section Three is a "How To" section of the book where we will bring home the points reinforced in the first two sections using some stories that illustrate key Agile Thinking points. This section should drive enough activity to turn a thought exercise into thought leadership, which will build upon your cocktail party genius and make you the hero at home or at work that you've always wanted to be (actually, it won't, but if it makes you happier and more productive, we will all collectively celebrate this as a win).

Like a lot of other works on the subject, this book represents the author's take on a very transformative movement. It is not meant to minimize or otherwise discredit those who developed the methodology, nor does it mean to discredit any professional currently utilizing Agile in the field for which it was originally intended. In fact, I would like to think that those brave people who started the movement would smile on the fact that we're trying to take their hard work improving software development and turning their collective vision into a hard, practical reality for everyday folks like you and me.

I hope this book educates a little, inspires a bit, and changes a lot for the better. As you read through it, think of other ways in which this type of practice can apply to your life or to the lives of others, and don't be afraid to share along the way. After all, we are a collection of individuals who interact. We care about our end results. We focus on collaboration and try our damndest to respond to the changes that life throws at us. We are humans just trying to overcome life's challenges (be they personal or professional), achieve greater efficiency (working smarter, not harder), or simply getting by (making sure everyone is fed, cleaning up the spilled milk on the floor, and getting everyone to a hockey practice that started twenty minutes ago).

It is your life. Now let's try to make it easier, together.

Ever forward,

Jack

SECTION ONE:

THE MOVEMENT

If you are living a life that has any element of complexity in it whatsoever, then Agile is the answer to your prayers.

I don't care what you do, where you are, or in which profession you choose to collect your pay. There are always new ways to do things, processes to continuously improve, and some external demand that requires us to move better, smarter, or faster. If you're in software or product development, then your work is tied to a market need that is defined by your users. If you're a parent, then you understand the main tasks required to get your kids to their activities in ways that result in minimized stress levels for you (that don't include wine). If you work in construction, maybe you see a need to maximize efficiency without compromising worker safety. All of these personas or scenarios are valid reasons for trying to apply Agile to your dailies.

In this section, we will review several ways in which to create your "Agile Thinking Self." Building your best "Agile Thinking Self" may require a fundamental shift in the way that you approach your work, your relationships, or other parts of your personal lives. We'll read a bit about the circumstances under which the movement (known as Agile, our umbrella term that refers to a number of different tools and processes used to build working software more effectively) was created, pressure test the principles within the bounds of our day-to-day grind, and then begin to piece together the theories so that we can apply them regularly.

Speaking of piecing things together, I love to use the concept of a bridge as a metaphor to drive home my Agile teaching. For our purposes here, think of this book as a bridge that takes you from your current place in life to a new, hopefully more organized existence. The overall composition of the bridge is entirely up to you—whether it is a very flexible (but functional) rope bridge, or a totally overengineered behemoth of stone, steel, and concrete—the fundamental purpose of either structure is to get you where you need to go.

The bridge concept is a big thing in my house. As a father of four children ranging in age from college to grade school, I am always trying to give coaching and life lessons to set them up for their futures. I want them to be their own people—good people—so I am very choosy about the lessons I impart to them as a father and as a leader. The guidance we give our kids forms a bridge that, due to generational differences, changing life circumstances, and so on, will only apply so much. Our kids will remember our words about how to get where they're ultimately going, but they will have to build their own life experiences to teach future generations how to live, love, and succeed. After all, are we parents not bridges? We take the lessons our parents gave us and try our hardest to connect them to the lessons our kids are learning in this modern age. Trust me, we're bridging.

In a similar vein, my professional life is currently built on imparting my knowledge to the next generation of leaders, as I have successfully (but not gracefully) moved from Analyst or "New Guy," to "person with an office" or "someone's boss." I want to make sure that my successors learn what I learned, but only enough to build their own careers on their own ideas. This is, in my opinion, one of the things that makes the rat race worth running: watching those who come after us surpass us in achievement or thought leadership. Bridge on.

This is more than just the intent of this book, folks—this will be the central focus of our journey together. Let's look at ways to take the knowledge that the founders of this great movement learned as they went through their thought process and begin to form opinions on how best to improve life for you and for others.

Ever forward!

CHAPTER ONE:

THE SCIENCE BEHIND THE AGILE THINKER

———

Keeping a bridge in good working order is serious business. One missed round of maintenance could be the difference between crossing over safely (good thing) and taking an involuntary swim (bad thing).

Continuing the reflection on bridges reminds me of one of the engineering marvels of the modern world, the Chesapeake Bay Bridge Tunnel (or, CBBT, for those of you familiar with the vernacular). The tunnel is a twenty-mile stretch of bridge and tunnels that connects Virginia's eastern shore with the metro areas of seven cities—an area known locally as Hampton Roads. (By the by, there will be a trivia question for you at some point... the cities are Norfolk, Suffolk, Portsmouth, Hampton, Chesapeake, Virginia Beach, and Newport News). The CBBT is a bridge-tunnel that crosses the *entire* span of the lower Chesapeake Bay.

I first encountered the CBBT as a newly minted Ensign in the Navy. My ever-faithful Volkswagen Jetta and I were fresh out of my first training duty station in Newport, Rhode Island, and cutting a path south to my first actual port home of Norfolk, Virginia. The last leg of the journey required me to cross the Bridge Tunnel, and given that I left Newport late in the morning, it was pitch dark by the time I crossed. A few things to note:

1. Your ability to see past the horizon is typically eleven to twelve miles at sea level;

2. As mentioned above, the bridge-tunnel is twenty miles long; so, therefore...

3. There is a point during the crossing when you can *barely* see lights from either shore, which is usually enough to freak most people out, or at a minimum give you the creeps.

In my opinion, it is one of the most amazing engineering feats that we've accomplished as a country—right up there with reversing the flow of the Chicago River, building the Hoover Dam, and developing our national Interstate System. The most amazing thing about the CBBT, though, is the schedule for preventive maintenance that the structure undergoes to keep it in good working order for those commuting over and through it. Since the Chesapeake Bay is home to a lot of large-draft merchant shipping traffic, large bridges can be a hazard, so there are mile-long tunnels that extend under the major shipping lanes (fun fact: I've actually driven ships over the Thimble Shoals tunnel in the CBBT).

Considering the fact that the CBBT has concrete and steel bridge structures planted in very corrosive saltwater coupled with two tunnels that require similar protection from the elements plus ventilation so that vehicle exhaust can be removed, you have quite the issue, maintenance-wise. For example, painting the tunnel—one of the work streams that makes up a part of the maintenance plan for the structure— is done throughout the year to offset some of the corrosive effects of saltwater, rough seas, and structural wear and tear. This means that maintaining the bridge-tunnel is a yearly evolution with daily tasks. If a paint crew starts painting the tunnel on January 1, they don't theoretically finish painting until December 31—right about the time when it's time to start painting again.

Talk about job security: this is a complex effort that requires structure and discipline, but if you're a contracting company working on painting, your year is set! If we look deeply into the maintenance program of the CBBT—and I promise that we won't do that here—you'll find an intricate balance of dependencies, complexities, milestones, and deliverables. You'll see resources (people), equipment, consumables, even possibly food. All of these items need to fall into place for the CBBT crew to successfully perform its yearly (daily) preventive maintenance.

Looking broadly into the program we're focused on in this book, you begin to see the parallels between maintaining a twenty-mile long bridge-tunnel and the complexity found in our daily lives. I'm willing to bet that, regardless of your age/station/job/goals/circumstances, you have an intricate, yearly and daily balance of dependencies (tasks that need to be completed so that others may be done successfully), a lot of chaos involved with each (like ensuring that one child gets to her orchestra rehearsal and another makes it to Scouts, while the rest end up at soccer practice on the other side of town), important milestones (like remembering holidays, a friend's birthday, or your anniversary), and deliverables (submitting a sales or status report on time, completing carpentry work, turning in school permission slips, or washing the hook-and-ladder in the firehouse). Yikes.

Like the CBBT maintainers, we need a plan. Better yet, we need a system or a baseline of learning to manage, prioritize, and execute against all the work and chaos that life throws at us. We need to build and maintain our own Agile Thinking "bridge" so that we can figure life out, get stuff done, and take the last few steps to whatever supports our definition of progress or success.

For those in the business world, our needs are simple:

- We want to improve the value of the investment dollars that we sink into our company projects;
- We want greater integration amongst the solutions that we deploy to our customers so that we can run them more efficiently and with less cost;
- We want to bring products and services to our customers faster than we did last year (which is much easier said than done); and
- We want to increase the amount of collaboration within the four walls of our enterprise (among our employees) and outside the four walls of our enterprise (being more reactive to the needs and feedback of our customers).

In other words, we want to use our business dollars to ensure that we work on the top priority functions of a project to gain the most value; do our best to enable solutions that are scalable and flexible; and take advantage of shorter, more achievable batches of delivered items that will end up in the hands of our business and customers more frequently.

We want a better way of being, doing, delivering, and living.

To illustrate, we can look at how the art and science of software development have evolved so that we can see how Agile improves the way that work should be done. We can blend our figurative bridge example above with the reality of work practiced by software development practitioners ("developers") today. For the purposes of illustration, I would go so far as to say that both bridge maintainers and software developers alike share many of the same required needs. Additionally, bridge people and software people share a lot of the complexity that everyday humans (although they would like to think of themselves as superhuman, I'm sure <insert wink emoji here>) have in their lives.

Traditional software development as we know it started out in the defense sector in the 1960s (referred to loosely in this book and across industry as the "Waterfall" methodology). Waterfall is a very linear, sequential process that includes: (1) a way to ideate on and document what needs to be done (Requirements); (2) a process to put formal prototypes together of what the end product should look like (Design); (3) a phase that includes the actual work of developing the product (Development/Implementation); (4) a dedicated effort to test everything (Testing); and (5) a mechanism to make the code "live" for market use (Deployment). Waterfall, as a construct, gave stakeholders exactly what they needed at the time: a formalized, structured method of technical project management based on proven, traditional systems engineering practices. Using the phased process above, Waterfall modes of software development and project delivery became the standard. Teams began to drive their work by Documenting, Designing, Developing, Testing, and Deploying their wares to completion. It required a rigid adherence to process, excessive documentation tied to IT controls, and multiple decision checkpoints (called "gates") that allowed the team to continue forward through the various phases of the work effort.[3]

Well, you know what they say: "The best laid plans of mice and men oft go awry." Over time, some limitations of Waterfall began to surface: the phased approach takes too long; the level of rework is too high in later phases; the delivery dates can slip… and the list goes on.

Critics of the Waterfall methodology are all over the map with their dislikes: some don't want process for process' sake, others think that the sequential nature of delivery doesn't move quickly enough, and still others dislike the fact that multiple "handoffs" have to take place as the software or project takes shape (in other words, software testers may have an issue receiving a batch of code from the developers after they've finished coding). Learning about what was

---

3   Winston W. Royce, "Managing the Development of Large Software Systems," Paper presented at the meeting of the Proceedings IEEE WESCON, 1970.

built, why it was built, and how it needs to be tested can be a complex series of tasks, so more transition time is definitely a good thing.

All of this boils down to one major question that has been on everyone's minds for decades: why should we be expected to create a complete set of requirements and design documentation at the start of the process when we know the absolute least about the end product?

In my simplified view, we shouldn't know everything up front, because that isn't how life works. Instead, an ideal process would allow us to start with what we do know, incorporate any learnings along the way, and then take the next steps to learning more about what we're building. As technology grew and the media through which we connected with customers became more available, our need to satisfy those whom we serve became paramount and did not lend itself well to linear, logical phases of delivery. Waterfall was becoming obsolete; in fact, there were two things missing from Waterfall that required a new way of thinking:

1. **Waterfall mandates that you predict everything about what you're going to build ("Requirements") at a time when you actually know the least about what the end result is ultimately going to look like. If you don't specialize in predicting the future with some degree of accuracy (and who does?), then this a pretty big problem.** How many times have you started a project at home, school, or work, only to get new asks or features along the way? My guess is that when the project completes—no

matter what the project was—the end product doesn't look *exactly* the way you envisioned it at the start.

2. **Waterfall doesn't typically include the end customer in the process until late into development—or, in some cases, toward the end of testing.** How many times have you completed a project in your house only to find out at the end that your spouse or partner had other ideas? This is how fights start.

Great context, I suppose, but the main question that often goes unanswered when debating which method of delivery is best is this: How can you follow a sequential process that assumes you will know everything at the point in the project when you actually know nothing, while ensuring that your end customers are happy and confident that the project will complete on time and to their ultimate satisfaction? The short answer? You can't.

To illustrate, imagine our intrepid crew working on the bridge-tunnel. It's cold, the Chesapeake Bay is spraying sea-water everywhere, and the workers just want to complete their daily tasks so they can go home and eat dinner. The crew in question—the painters, for example—have just finished half of their daily painting tasks, only to find that those who are responsible for preparing the surface for painting have not finished their tasks without telling the painters. This means that one group (the painters) can't begin their work until another group (those preparing the surface of the bridge for painting) complete theirs. Big problem. Delays ensue. Timelines slip. Tempers flare. Actual dinner at home gets cold for some, and for others the prospect of having dinner disappears completely. Disaster.

Their experience—in this case, one with a low level of collaboration, mismanagement of dependencies, and a lot of hurt feelings—resulted in a loss of productivity, happiness, and dinner.

Of course, this is just one example of where sequential processes can go drastically wrong if not managed effectively. As a matter of practice, we need to remember that sequential processes don't always work in the way that we like, thus making Mike Tyson's immortal words all the more true: "Everyone has a plan until they get punched in the mouth."[4]

Building the connective tissue between what a process says has to happen (like we do in Waterfall) and what common sense says has to happen *now* can be a bit of a departure.

There has to be a better way. There just *has* to.

Enter Agile. Our focus on the general notion that "there has to be a better way" of working begins with an industry-wide frustration with linear, sequential process. The very core concept of Agile, as the name implies, led the founders of that framework—seventeen intrepid souls that assembled in Snowbird, Utah, to find a better way of organizing and deploying software code—to begin writing a manifesto on how to work and operate better. While their primary focus

---

4   "Everyone has a plan until they get punched in the mouth." —Mike Tyson

was on getting software code to market more effectively and efficiently, they were also writing a blueprint for the rest of us.

By the by, it's not a figurative manifesto, it's an actual manifesto. Loosely referred to as "The Agile Manifesto." It reads:

"We are uncovering better ways of developing software by doing it and helping others do it. Through this work we have come to value:

Individuals and interactions *over processes and tools.*

Working software *over comprehensive documentation.*

Customer collaboration *over contract negotiation.*

Responding to change *over following a plan.*

That is, while there is value in the items on the right, we value the items on the left more."[5]

That's it. That's all it says.

Pound for pound, this is one of the most impactful yet simple ways of starting a movement. My read on the above is, "We're not telling you that all that you know is wrong. In fact, what we are simply saying is that it is more important to talk about what your objective is (what you want to build, code, or accomplish) and how you can get it done more simply in pieces than it is to try to tackle it all at once. It doesn't trash

---

5   "The Agile Manifesto," Agile Alliance, accessed July 20, 2020.

convention; it merely enhances it. The items in bold are not the only things that are important—just more important than the non-bolded, traditional ways of doing things."

Let's take a moment to unpack the Agile Manifesto line by line and see if we can relate to each of the points individually to begin applying them to our daily lives.

Individuals and interactions over processes and tools: According to the signers of the Manifesto, people write software, not the tools and processes themselves. Tools and processes are enablers: you pick your favorite and adjust your approach accordingly. The most important message here is to not go completely overboard on all the tools at your disposal, but to find new and innovative ways to get those around you to engage and help. We will endeavor to do this together in the chapters ahead.

Working software over comprehensive documentation: At my house, we got a new, fancy coffee maker last winter. As soon as we took the machine out of the box, we filed the instructions away, never to be seen again. How many times do you do that with your tools? You buy something new, you bring it home, and then you plug it in and try it yourself. I feel confident in saying that 90 percent of you do the same, because you have a clear idea of what needs to be done ("we need coffee'"), you have a machine that will help you do it (a fancy coffee maker), and your goal is to give it some electrical juice and figure it out yourselves. Even though this piece is about software, the principle still applies. The first measure of any software development project should be that the outcome or functionality—the stated, agreed-upon purpose for which the software was built in the first place—is completed and released. Our lives are no different. Now go get your coffee!

Customer collaboration over contract negotiation: Despite all of the technology that connects us, we live in an incredibly disconnected society. I am in the Generation X set (so not a "boomer," kids) and come from a time when interactions had to be interpersonal as opposed to the digital interactions we all have today. If you needed something, you picked up the phone or walked over to another human and asked for it. Now, we are so captivated by the six-inch screen that gives us text messages, movies, or (groan) our email that we rely on interpersonal communication less and less. I'm not saying that technology is bad, nor am I saying that millennials and Generations Y and Z need to get off of their phones; rather, I am saying that when it comes to getting something done quickly, a direct connection with a friend, partner, or coworker can make all the difference.

A quick example: think of your workplace. Historically, traditional companies were structured so that the resources—mainly, the people—were treated as expendable, interchangeable parts of a machine that, when used together, produced a product, delivered an outcome, or provided a service. An Agile organization is totally different. Agile thinkers use the power of personal connections to self-organize, discuss roadblocks, and solve problems in real time. Think about the last time you asked for help via e-mail. Did you get a response right away? If you did, did the person to whom you sent the message have enough context to give you exactly what you wanted? If the answer to those questions is "no," then consider yourself in good company. Agile Thinkers like us need to view our organizations (family, friend networks, or workplaces) as a system where people can connect, organize around a shared purpose, and solve problems in real time to produce a result.

And about the "get off your phone" thing: Actually, I *am* saying that we should all get off our phones. My commute to Chicago every day requires me to walk to and from a train station, and I would be rich if I had a dollar for every time I had to get out of the way of someone not paying attention because they were walking while simultaneously binge-watching their favorite show. Not to mention how many close calls I've witnessed where these same folks narrowly miss being clipped by a cab, CTA bus, or even an oncoming train. People—Get. Off. Your. Phones.

Responding to Change over Following a Plan: What's important is not *that* the work gets done, but *how* it gets done. In this day and age, we want to work smarter, not harder, right? The pace of life isn't slowing down; in fact, it's just the opposite. When you consider the obligations in your work life and combine them with your workload at home and in your personal life, it can be absolutely overwhelming. Our bet here—which aligns directly with what the founders of the Agile Manifesto were trying to achieve—is that people will instinctively try to find the most efficient way of completing a task. Our mission in this book will be to look at some techniques to help us all: focus on the simple, engage others as often as necessary, and think less about the plan than about the planning itself (you do need a plan, though, because a goal without a plan is just a wish). This is a great place to start, given that change is always a constant in our lives.

This last point—the part about responding to change—is going to be key to your ability to bond with this book. We are not looking for a new, wholesale self-help method to improve our lives. We are simply seeking to find new and innovative ways to make our lives easier to manage successfully. Using the bridge built by pieces of the Manifesto above, in whole or in part, will help us get there while (hopefully) keeping our sanity along the way.

CHAPTER TWO:

MAKING LIFE EASIER BY MASTERING YOUR WIP

———

I have a friend who famously said, "When you break it down into smaller pieces, even rocket science isn't rocket science." And he should know; he is a rocket scientist. Like, a real one. Rockets and everything.

This also reminds me of one of the principles that supports our manifesto: "Simplicity—the art of maximizing the amount of work not done—is essential."

Counterintuitively, in our minds the element of simplicity and the engineering discipline of rocket science will go hand in hand. In fact, as a matter of practice, we are going to build the muscle memory required to take the inordinate amount of complexity that life throws at us and crush the daylights out of it by making our chaotic, complex lives easier to understand. Keeping things simple and efficient will be paramount as we move forward in this journey together, so please keep an open mind—this is important. Even if we're tasked with building rockets!

Simplicity is a commodity that is increasingly hard to come by these days. No matter where you turn—from getting kids on a school bus on time each morning to building or maintaining a bridge across the Chesapeake Bay—we need a ton of moving parts to fall into place so that our mornings can be deemed successful. Considering the age-old question of "how does one eat an elephant?" and applying the somewhat cheeky answer of "one bite at a time," we can begin to put our complexity into perspective.

The Agile Manifesto we just reviewed in the previous chapter makes a bold statement on how we, as humans, can begin to view our own brand of complexity in a different light. By placing a new emphasis on how we involve others, focusing on what we know needs to be completed, and then being open to change as we engage our resources, we can start to take tasks head on, one small piece at a time. By focusing on a few new (but basic) principles like work in process (WIP), simplifying flow, and managing our exit rate, we can reduce tasks that were once seemingly insurmountable and make them easier for us to digest and complete. Let's begin.

NOW WIP IT! WIP IT GOOD!

Consider one of the most easily relatable complex tasks that we face: holiday shopping. If you have a family like mine, this is one of the best and worst times of the year. *Christmas Vacation* is on TV, trees are up, holiday cheer abounds, but for me understanding the needs of seven people—all uniquely important and critical stakeholders—on top of my other personal and professional responsibilities feels like a heavy weight placed upon my shoulders. I simultaneously love and hate the holidays, and that's a problem.

It really shouldn't be that way, but this is our reality. I blame retailers that begin stocking shelves with holiday stuff and playing holiday songs as I am walking my jack o'lantern to the curb after Halloween. At least I can cram down some peppermint bark or some kind of fancy holiday latte (or spiked eggnog, Griswold style) to help deal with the stress!

In reality, though, holiday shopping in our house is a big deal. Every November, we get our kids together at a local Starbucks, buy them some kind of holiday-themed hot chocolate, and get them to write out their lists for the big day in December. The output of the exercise is interesting: the net result is a number of items, ranging from the least specific from my oldest child (hockey gear) to the laser accuracy of my youngest child (giant sloth stuffed animal, scented markers, solution to climate change). So some inputs are specific, some not, and when considered in conjunction with the other gift requirements for other family members, friends, and coworkers, we get a somewhat decent idea as to the magnitude of our shopping problem (Hint: it's big).

As parents, my wife and I could choose to add up all of the items on the list, prioritize by date needed (because family get-togethers and office parties are well before the actual holidays), and begin to tick items off one by one until the list is complete. However, with seven people in our house plus the shopping needs of extended family and coworkers, the list becomes less of a straightforward exercise and more of a dynamic, ever-changing source of anxiety for my wife and me. Every year, we need a way to make constant, incremental improvement to our shopping requirements while reducing the amount of stress it places on us as we address the obligations in our day jobs.

Never underestimate the impact of multiple To-Do lists! While it's great to have all of your thoughts on paper somewhere, having multiple lists for different stakeholders all over the place can put quite a strain on you and your mental health. Like our holiday shopping lists, we need a way to organize and simplify the items while at the same time regulate the amount of time and effort it takes to tick them off the list.

We need to look at the volume of our obligations and determine the best way to accommodate those obligations. We need to take charge of our situation and reduce our work in progress, or our WIP. WIP is a productivity killer if not managed correctly. So, what if I told you that what we need in this case is to whip our WIP?

<Insert cracking sound.>

Before we whip anything, we need to first understand what WIP is and why it is relevant to our lives. As mentioned above, WIP—or our work in process—has a huge impact on our ability to focus. It can be not only be a constraint on your ability to get things done, but it can also be one of your biggest assets as an Agile Thinker. For the purposes of our discussion here, let's do a quick exercise: I want you to think of everything you have to do in your personal and professional life. If you're like the majority of Americans, you most likely envisioned your professional To-Do list first (which is a shame, but normal in this day and age). For example, if you're in sales, chances are that monthly reports are coming due; if you work on the CBBT, then bridge maintenance schedules need to be completed (please don't slow the painters down!); and if you're a first responder, maybe the fire engine needs to be cleaned today. Now, overlay those professional tasks with all the other stuff that is being thrown at you in your personal life: perhaps you're taking care of an elderly parent, or you need to advocate for a child who is having trouble in school. Maybe you're behind on laundry and the dog is running out of food. Also, hockey practice started ten minutes ago and your thirteen-year-old can't find her skates. It's a mess.

Now, let's continue our exercise by looking at all of the items that are in process now. On the professional side, you may have a working draft of that sales report, you're in the process of completing the paperwork for your struggling student, and you're wrangling your kids into the car for practice. All of that in-flight activity is WIP.

Many organizations—be they companies, work teams, first responder squads, or even families—operate by managing WIP. A lot of teams working in managing supply chains or developing new software or technology consider the reduction of WIP as a sign of progress and efficiency. It demonstrates the team or organization is heading toward a stated objective or vision with as few barriers to success as possible. By limiting our work in process, we are able to improve flow (the amount of work that we are able to handle and sustain as efficiently as possible) on a daily basis. This is a really important concept for us as Agile Thinkers to understand.

A quick, very relevant example: Disney monitors WIP constantly. If you have ever been to a Disney theme park during the summer months, you have seen the impact of WIP by standing in line for one of the more popular attractions. They are excellent at keeping the lines moving at an optimal pace for the patrons and employees alike. They are constantly analyzing ways to make sure that hot and tired parents are able to manage expectations of their kids, who are also hot and tired (and *way* less patient). Essentially, Disney believes that reducing the time to go through lines (again, in a way that makes the most sense for patrons and employees) is paramount. They use a process improvement theorem called "Little's Law" that focuses on process lead time (which is the time you spend waiting in line) as a function of controlling the WIP for their attractions (the number of people ahead of you) and their output (the flow of people enjoying the rides, then leaving). If they optimize their WIP by managing the amount of time people wait in line, more happy riders will process efficiently through the rides with minimal levels of screaming by tired, impatient children (or, tired, impatient adults—we grown-ups can get lost in our emotions as well, especially if the line to Space Mountain doesn't move!).[6]

Understanding this concept is an important lever in our ability to organize our commitments, deliver on our promises,

6   RCI Consulting, "Little's Law at Disney," November 23, 2013, Video, 1:56; J.D.C. Little, "A Proof for the Queuing Formula: $L = \lambda W$," *Operations Research*. 9, no. 3 (1961): 383–387.

and just make our lives easier. Let's go back to our holiday shopping commitments, since at the time of writing they remain very front of mind. My wife and I have a WIP issue: we have a short lead time, a significant number of items to buy for seven people, and a requirement for a high exit rate to get through our list. Since we are comfortable with the items we know (the WIP), we can begin to focus on our next variable—the flow management that will help us make the most out of our already short lead time.

FINDING YOUR CENTER BY REDUCING WIP

Reducing your personal WIP can be done by first breaking down the work into small, manageable chunks that can be organized, prioritized, and grouped so that you (or others) can execute them. This is where each of us can take what we thought was "rocket science" and make it "not-so rocket sciencey." The act of simplifying those tasks that seem too large, too stressful, or just too much is less of an art and more of a science—especially when you consider how your work seems to pile up in your life. We refer to this "piling up" phenomenon as "queueing." Looking back to the exercise we ran through earlier, I want you to reconsider the lists of things you have going on in your work and personal life. Think of the items that are on your To-Do list today. Without a doubt, you have several work-related items to accomplish, multiple projects around the house that need to be completed, and possibly myriad child obligations as well. Oh, and a grocery list? Check. Need to get the cat to the vet? Of course. Teeth need to be cleaned? Sure. If any of this resonates with your current life experience, you are living a life that needs some WIP reduction.

In reality, reducing personal WIP is no different than using the methodologies that Disney uses to reduce wait times for their attractions (though you can always address the problem by spending the extra dollars on a Fast Pass). We will look at the mechanics of reducing WIP in later chapters, but before we get into the ones and zeroes of what WIP is and why it's important to reduce, we will need to get our minds right. Think of this as an opportunity to meditate on how best to reduce your personal To-Do lists and how to make checking all the items contained on them easier. WIP yoga, if you will.

So get on your mat, find your center, and breathe. We're about to examine some tips that will allow you to better manage your life and keep your efficiency, effectiveness, and personal stress in line. Consider the following, for starters:

1. **Write it out, Kanban style.** There is a process called *Kanban* (Japanese for "card you can see," or "signboard") that can be an amazing Agile Thinking tool for us to use in this book and elsewhere. Kanban is a visual system that triggers an action. Kanban puts continuous improvement as a focus, manages the flow of work, and focuses on limiting the work in process.[7] It's awesome, and relatively easy. Want to get started? Good.

   To get moving with Kanban like a pro, start by creating a three-column list that captures your work items, tracks your progress, and lists all of the tasks that you completed along the way. Use an application like Trello

---

7   Taiichi Ōno, *Toyota Production System: Beyond Large-scale Production* (Cambridge, Mass: Productivity Press, 1988).

to create an online, shareable version of your list. My family uses Trello because it gives us the ability to enter small tasks that can be tracked by date, have all kinds of amplifying information in a comments section, and can be moved from a column labeled "'To Do" to a column labeled "WIP," and, universe-willing, to a column labeled "Complete." Trello is great because it can also be accessed via your phone or tablet, which is super convenient if you are out at a store shopping. Of course, you don't have to use Trello; some people are more comfortable with creating a large space on a wall at home that has handwritten post-it notes with things they have to do. Either method is very effective—the key here is to get your thoughts down and give yourself the ability to track progress from what is stacking up in your "To-Do" column, manage the work in your "WIP" column, and hopefully celebrate the tasks that show up in your "Complete" column.

2. **Find your velocity!** Velocity, in software development, is loosely defined as a measure of how much work a team can accomplish over a period of time. There is some good news and bad news here, so because we Agile Thinkers meet problems head on, we'll start with the bad news first: before we can move into a full, Agile Thinking mode, we need to become comfortable with the concept of velocity. Unfortunately, determining velocity is difficult, even for professional software development teams. In order to determine their velocity, newly formed teams have to employ a bit of trial and error until they have spent enough time working to be able to measure how much work they can achieve in a day (or in a two-week period). Velocity is based on how much work they were able to

complete, not the amount of work they took on. Their struggle is real, and you will face the same challenge.

Now, the good news: as Agile Thinkers we can start simple and allow ourselves to experiment a bit before we calculate anything. Hooray for experimentation and the allowable failure that tends to result from it! Actually, let's start now—I want you to take a minute and reflect on all the items on your personal and professional To-Do lists again. Once you have a good idea as to how your combined To-Do list looks, think about how much you think you can reasonably complete in one day. Take some focused time—say, an hour during lunch, three hours on a weekend, or ten minutes while waiting for your evening train—and come up with a number (in hours) to plan your productivity for each day of the week. This will allow you to set reasonable goals for yourself every day and will help you to better engage others who can potentially help you complete your work. Engaging other resources is a big accelerator to your productivity; because others can complement your efforts by focusing their strengths on components of your work where your skills aren't as sharp. Teamwork does, in fact, make the dream work!

3. **Measure, then manage what you measure.** Spend time every day measuring how effective you are at planning your day and how accurate you're starting to get in planning the amount of time it takes you to complete items on your To-Do list. Additionally, always monitor the amount of work coming in to your To Do list and the amount of time items tend to sit there. We'll get into this later, but you can learn a lot about yourself, your limitations,

and any areas that require improving by measuring these two time metrics. Focus on your velocity first, though, as this will drive your ability to be proficient in many other modes of Agile Thinking.

4. **Be honest.** Be transparent with yourself about your workload. Ask yourself what you've been doing since the prior day, what you'll be working on today, and identify any obstacles that may lie in your path. This will allow you to engage in what I like to call "management by passive aggression," where, in a team environment, the team members will push a member that gives the same status several days in a row. The same dynamic will apply to your own internal dialogue as well. If you're thinking about the same things that are open on your list day after day, ultimately you're going to feel guilty enough to push those things over the finish line. Be honest with yourself and dedicate your mind to completing your work. The rest will follow.

To lay the foundations for Agile Thinking, you need to understand your ability to deliver and measure your completion rate—always. Be honest, be vulnerable, and be open to feedback (whether it be from your own, internal dialogue or feedback provided by others).

Easy enough, right? Sure. Now, let's look at some more technical ways to dig a little deeper.

IS LEANER BETTER?

In operating efficiency, yes; in bacon, no. *Lean* enterprises are those companies that utilize the continuous improvement discipline called "Lean" where the core idea is to maximize *customer value* (the best possible outcome from customers or stakeholders) while minimizing *waste* (non-essential tasks, or those things that you do during the day that don't directly contribute to you being effective). Simply put, being Lean means creating more value for customers with fewer resources, and if you are a company that actively and expertly practices Lean, your employees will tend to think this way all of the time. In a Lean enterprise, the company tries to realize a state of "continuous flow," where items are manufactured, software code built, or just work in general moves more quickly across its lines of production and into the hands of its customers or stakeholders. Lean enterprises look to empower all employees to spot inefficiencies and suggest improvements and think in small batch sizes (smaller units of work) to create greater predictability in delivery. Why? Well, they a) are most likely looking to do the right amount of work for the most amount of efficiency; b) have to answer to stakeholders, or in the case of public companies, stockholders; or c) have a reason to do both a) and b) and may also seek perfection in everything that they do. I will buy all three, but my option d) is because they are managed by human beings. A Lean enterprise is not Lean necessarily because of the continuous improvement methodology it adopts, but because it is managed by human beings who just want to do things better. I would even go so far as to say that all of those human beings are Agile Thinking individuals, whether they know it or not! If someone could please welcome them to the Agile Thinking family, I would be very grateful. Go ahead—I'll wait.

The point? As an individual, you're a Lean enterprise and you don't even know it! Do you look for shorter routes on your commute that get you to work faster or save gas? Do you lay out your clothes the night before so that your morning is easier to handle? Do you question everything in an attempt to find the best answer, the best solution, or the best way forward through a problem?

Well, do you? (Sorry, that was me questioning everything.)

Of course you do! You're human and are therefore primed to recognize both your most valuable and your least impactful solution to just about any problem (unless you work for the Internal Revenue Service—we'll convert you guys yet).

Your Lean and WIP-reducing thought exercise should focus on your flow: making sure that you are doing just enough to keep yourself productive without stopping. This will make you feel as if you are accomplishing something all of the time and will mitigate the impact of the anxiety you feel when you have a large, overloaded To-Do list. So let's look at our next concept, flow.

GO WITH THE FLOW

Adults have a lot of obligations and can be overloaded very easily. Think about a stressful time of the year—be it tax time (tip of the cap to the snarky IRS comment above), a family vacation planning cycle (we freak out having to pack for seven people), or holiday shopping. Your call. Now think about a time when you had so much on your plate that life almost seemed too difficult to manage. Again, I'll wait while you think about that... Back? Good. My guess is that you came up with several examples. It seems that getting ourselves overloaded to the point where life seems unmanageable is an increasingly common problem these days. In order to make everything seem easier and make good on our commitments to ourselves and to others, we will use our four WIP yoga items outlined above to achieve the following:

1. *Visualize, understand and get comfortable* with our WIP (work in process), and apply our WIP to our To-Do lists.

2. Break our big-ticket items on our To-Do lists into chunks that are *smaller* and *easier to handle.*

3. *Manage* the queue length, or the time it takes to organize, line up by priority, and ultimately process your list items.

Success here requires us to take each of these items and use it to revisit the WIP yoga thought exercise we did earlier. Visualizing your WIP is best done using a simple, easily understandable method of controlling the items on your list. For starters, organize your list and make it visible. Use a three-column list or use Trello as described while we were doing our first pose in WIP yoga. Remember to display the work you or your team signed up to do, the work currently in process, and the work that has been completed.

Take a few minutes to write down all of the items on your To-Do list, and then create entries for your status board (in

Trello, on your wall, or on your cat—it doesn't matter). Then take a few minutes to review each one and break it into items that you can typically do in a day or less. If, for example, your list has "Complete draft text of *The Agile Thinker* book," then you may want to think about creating items like "Complete introduction of *The Agile Thinker* book," or "Call publisher and beg for exposure of *The Agile Thinker* book." Speaking from experience, these are items that can be done in a day; the former was an actual item on my board, and the latter is a regularly recurring fixture.

Once you have broken up your items into smaller pieces, or "chunks" (to use the technical term), you are ready to begin organizing your life. On your board, create a "card" to represent each of the smaller chunks and place them at the far left of your board. This will serve as the To-Do pile, where you will nearly faint due to all the items placing demands on your life. Take a deep breath, then move one—just one—item into the next column to the right. This is your "In Process" or "WIP" column.

Congratulations! You are now an Agile-thinking, Kanban-practicing machine! You're on your way to fame, fortune, process excellence, and personal fulfillment! While I can't guarantee the first two, I can certainly hope for the last two.

At any rate, once that first item is moved into the "WIP" or "In Process" column, pay close attention to how long it takes you to complete it. This is the opportunity for you to understand your "personal velocity" as described above. The amount of work you can do in a day is something that will help you move the items from the left side of your board to the "Complete" side of your board, and through this velocity number you will understand how long it will take to exhaust the items on your list. You need to be careful here, because if you are optimizing WIP, you need to understand one important law of WIPing:

"When any workflow state reaches its WIP limit, no new work is taken on. This matches demand to capacity and increases flow through the system."[8]

What the quote above means for people like you and me is this: If you have a lot of items waiting to start and have several items that are in process and are taking longer than anticipated, you should reconsider before adding new items—or, consider hiring an assistant. Your call. Check in with yourself constantly. Reviewing your board daily and thinking about what was done yesterday, what will be done today, and what obstacles lie in your path will help you gain clarity on your life's obligations and help you execute them more quickly. This is something that teams use to create transparency and honesty across the team itself, so that the team can become more productive. It totally works, even if you're a team of one!

NETTING IT OUT

Limiting your WIP may seem counterintuitive. The natural tendency for any busy person is to assume that the more work you put into your flow, the more you should get accomplished.

---

8   "Principle #6—Visualize and limit WIP, reduce batch sizes, and manage queue lengths," Scaled Agile, Inc., accessed July 21, 2020.

This is not necessarily true. That logic fails the minute you identify an obstacle, a blocker to your progress, or some dependency (i.e. we cannot make the rocket fly until it is fueled. And it does us no good to fuel a rocket without an engine). If you are excellent at identifying every element that you will need to be successful in completing your To-Do list and don't operate at the right level of productivity that your body, soul, and brain will allow, you will at best have a turbulent week trying to accomplish everything and, at worst, lose all productivity in your system by remaining busy the whole time but finishing nothing. For many people this may require us to say "no" to things that are unnecessary, especially if they are not crucial or job-related. Anything that doesn't produce value is waste. Managing your WIP by eliminating waste and watching flow is paramount, and it should be a primary focus for you. You can do it—I have total faith.

We will go more into Little's Law (that law used by Disney) a little more in this book, but remembering how it works will keep the items on your To-Do list or Trello board moving at the best rate possible. The law states that "the average wait time for service from a system equals the ratio of the average queue (To-Do list) length divided by the average processing rate." Assuming an average processing rate, the longer the line, the longer the wait. Space Mountain or any Starbucks at 8:30 a.m. will illustrate this point very, very well.

So if longer queues of work translate directly to longer wait times, either the length of the queue needs to be reduced or the rate of accomplishment needs to increase. In other words, get a shorter, more manageable list or get faster at achieving it. Visualizing the work as described here helps immensely.

So take a breath and remember our WIP yoga class. If we are able to visualize the work that needs to be done, understand the rate at which our To-Do items arrive and are completed, and understand completely how to take large, complex chunks of work and turn them into several smaller, more manageable chunks of work, then we will see a greater sense of control and improvements in how we get things done. Once mastered, we should attain a greater sense of engagement in our lives by owning both our workload and our productivity.

That goes even for you, rocket scientists!

SECTION TWO:

THE FOUNDATIONS

As the saying goes, a journey of a thousand miles begins with a single step. (Or, maybe it was never judge a person until you walk a mile in his shoes, because then you'll be a mile away and you'll have their shoes, but I digress.)[9]

Adjusting your way of thinking as a part of a broader, more comprehensive change to your daily work can be a long and difficult journey. In this section we will endeavor to focus on the next, single step you will need to take as a starting point to effecting that broad, transformative change.

Section Two focuses on some fundamental tools you can use to start your transition to becoming an Agile Thinker. For

---

9   "Before you criticize a man, walk a mile in his shoes. That way, when you do criticize him, you'll be a mile away and have his shoes." —Steve Martin

many of you, the tools you choose will be few in number. For others, you may wish to jump in with both feet and use as many as this book (and to be fair, scads of other sources out there) recommends. It doesn't matter. If you can take one thing away from this book, apply it to your life, and receive benefit from it, then that's a huge win for all of us. Agile Thinking never limits itself to any checklist, and neither should you!

We'll start slowly by focusing on how we view time, size, and the rates at which work arrives on our To-Do lists. As we progress through this section together, the most important thing for you to do is to visualize how the material discussed applies to your life, work, or family. I'd be willing to bet that in many cases, you will see a direct application, and in most cases, you will have plenty of takeaways to make at least a part of your life better. Again, win-win.

This is the "art" behind your Agile Thinking self as opposed to the "science" that we briefly looked at in Section One. Think of the material in this chapter as the ways in which an average person—just like you and me—can begin to apply Agile Thinking in our daily lives.

Turn the page and let's take that first step together!

CHAPTER THREE:

MAKING THE LEAP: BECOMING AN AGILE THINKER

For many of us, change is difficult. Like death and taxes, change is one of the very few things in life that is a constant throughout our days. In many ways, though, change can be an asset. In change lie myriad opportunities to discover what went right with our past, what didn't work so well, and what we can focus on going forward.

The reason why so many companies adopted Agile is precisely the same reason we're talking about it today: they saw a need to do things better, be more productive, or get products to market faster. They saw in themselves a much better future made possible by transforming their operations. Their experience, coupled with my experience leading these transformations, is a big reason why I wrote this book. If they can do it, why can't we? I would like to do things better. I would be all about being able to do things faster. I would love to "work smarter, not harder" to the extent that I can. I'm sure you have similar goals or want the same thing, so what could possibly be standing in the way?

Change. How we hate it so! The ever-present fear of change is the one thing that can kill the best ideas, laying waste to a gilded future paved with the smooth stones of dreams and possibilities. In business, we refer to change as one of those potentially negative elements in transforming from one way of business to another; one of those "organizational antibodies" that could attack and even bury your project and ultimately your credibility as a change leader.

The good news is that the only person you need to impress while reading this book is yourself. If you see an opportunity in your life to streamline the way you live, work, or interact with others, then consider making the leap to adopt some of the principles here. If you are the type of person who loves to plan, work your plan, and check your progress against said plan, you are also perfect for this book. In my humble opinion, if you have a pulse and have more going on in your life besides breathing and eating, then you are also eligible for what we're discussing. It's an elite group, no doubt.

COMPANIES CHANGE TO TRANSFORM FOR THE BETTER—AND SO SHOULD WE.

Let's continue our journey by getting in the right frame of mind. According to the Scrum Alliance, most companies choose to move to Agile as a delivery framework or way for teams to work for a few, very simple reasons:

- In software development, by focusing on the highest priority chunks of functionality, they can be assured that their workers are delivering the items that give them a maximum return on their investment;
- Agile helps businesses innovate more quickly, as you always focus on small batches, deliver the most important items first, collaborate openly, and continuously focus on what works well, what doesn't work well, and what the teams should focus on in their next delivery cycle. This concept, called a "retrospective," tends to unearth some pretty amazing ideas;
- Agile helps the company turn ideas into delivered product more quickly (but is not necessarily cheaper). One of the most common misconceptions of implementing Agile is that it is faster, cheaper, and better. Unfortunately, reality dictates that you can only pick two of those;
- Agile can provide a team with valuable insight into what customers want, thereby driving higher customer satisfaction; and
- The collaborative nature of Agile, combined with the fact that people are engaged throughout the project, drives better employee engagement and morale.[10]

WHY YOU SHOULD TRANSFORM TOO

Breaking this list down further, which, if any, of these items can apply to an individual? Well, if we were to rewrite the

---

10   Scrum Alliance, Inc. "Overview: What is Scrum?" Accessed July 21, 2020.

list above in a way that is less industry jargon and more from the perspective of an individual, it would read something like this:

- I need to make sure that my time is spent working on only those things that matter the most to me, my job, and my loved ones.
- I would like to begin engaging with the right resources that can help solve my problems or achieve my tasks and goals, and want to look for ways to do it better in the future.
- I want to get stuff done. Period.
- I want to be a person who is looked upon as someone who does the right things and does things right (which is a primary reason why we're going through this book together, am I right?).
- I want to make people happy by not overburdening them with how busy I am (once they see how engaged I am with life in general, I know just the book I can buy for them to make them more effective)!

OK, so the last one is a bit of a leap, but you know what? I had the opportunity and I took it. Can't blame a guy for trying.

Seriously, though, thinking through the reasons why a company would transform itself will align very well with your own personalized reasons for doing the same.

TAKING THE LEAP: GETTING STARTED
WITH YOUR NEW LIFE

I'll draw a parallel between the reason you're reading this book and some work that I did for a Fortune 500 building materials manufacturer. The company, headquartered in Chicago, is a leading manufacturer of building products. In fact, if you put down this book and look around at the walls surrounding you, there is a fair chance that you're staring at one of their signature products right now (if you're outside reading this, then good for you!). The Chief Information Officer (CIO) of this company approached me to propose a transformation of his IT delivery, saying the following:

- He desired an assessment of his IT organization's ability to deliver its products and solutions to stakeholders faster and more efficiently;
- His current method of delivery was way too entrenched in process-heavy, sequential (Waterfall) delivery, which did not meet the needs of his business partners, and transitively, their customers; and
- He wanted to make good on his vision to change the IT department's operating model so that he can improve customer satisfaction, increase his efficiency, and provide a clear and repeatable framework for the execution of his projects.

This is a typical ask. Most senior executives, including and especially the CIOs, want this level of visibility into how their departments deliver, as any improvements made inside the department can translate directly to happier customers, increased profits, or reduced overhead—all things that a Chief *Anything* Officer would want on his or her resume before moving into the next chapter of their careers.

I was initially excited at the prospect of working with this company, as all my previous transformation work centered on or around more technology-focused companies. Why on earth would a building manufacturer want to improve the way it produces code? I had to find out, so I got to work.

After producing the usual set of strategy deliverables: the current state assessment (here is where your company is today), the future state model (here is where your company really should be in the near future), and a whole host of supporting analyses, frameworks, and Agile training classes, I found what this company wanted to achieve for its IT department was not unlike what I wanted to achieve personally.

I wanted to empower my friends and associates to make better decisions. I wanted to be transparent enough with those around me so that they could see what I was doing and how I was doing it. I wanted to make my stakeholders—those at work and those at home—happier. I wanted to be more effective and efficient. These thoughts led me to put pen to paper and were main drivers of why you and I are here today.

The transformation project was successful not because of the pristine, flawlessly executed deliverables listed above (cough). It was successful because the company admitted it had issues and made the affirmative choice to take a leap.

This is what we all need to do daily. Various sources of research show that the average adult makes around 35,000 decisions a day, thereby confirming one of my favorite old adages that "life is a series of choices." That old saying is true, and given the complexities that life tends to throw at us during our adult years, we need a better way of being and doing.

I encourage you to pause and reflect on the CIO's ask, and try to draw parallels to your own life. Do you want to know how effective you are at your job or running your household? Do you feel that, despite your level of comfort with how you do things today, there may be a better way of doing them? Do you want to be able to increase levels of satisfaction amongst your family, friends, coworkers, and superiors? I'm guessing there are lots of "yes" answers across the board, which means only one thing: it's time to take the leap and make your own transformation happen.

Remember that the only person whom you need to impress in this transformative journey you're about to take is you. You are going to be the one who aligns on a strategy and navigates through it. You will be the person who will build self-sufficiency in your new way of being and doing by using some of the tools in this book. You will be the one who governs how you work, identifies ways to improve, and accelerate the areas of your life that you want to accelerate. Borrowing some of the pirate's words from that Tom Hanks movie, "you are the captain now."[11]

---

11   Paul Greengrass, Billy Ray, Scott Rudin, Dana Brunetti, Michael De Luca, Gregory Goodman, Eli Bush, *Captain Phillips*, Culver City, CA: Sony Pictures Home Entertainment (Firm), 2014.

STEPS TO ACHIEVING SUCCESS IN YOUR JOURNEY

My hope, captain, is that as you read through this book you will identify with some of the methods, stories, and tools that I have used or seen in the past. To better enable you to equip yourself with the right tools and techniques, I am going to give you the same high-level framework that ultimately became the recommendation for the building materials company.

My recommended way forward for the CIO was framed out in five steps:

- **Align the Organization**—Ensure that there is a clearly articulated change strategy in place, and empower a team to effectively make the change happen.
- **Define the Governance**—"Governance" typically refers to the management framework that an organization uses to make decisions and complete projects. Doing this well allows for organizations to better monitor performance, make the right decisions, and efficiently involve only those decision makers who need to impart the change.
- **Build Your Capabilities**—Define, refine, and build new processes, and seek to implement a framework for initial training and continuing education for all those affected.
- **Identify Accelerators**—An accelerator is any tool, technique, or process to help make a business function or task run faster or better.
- **Build Your Backlog**—We'll get into the concept of backlogs a bit later, but essentially a backlog is a list with items that can be constantly reviewed, prioritized, reprioritized, and deprioritized. It serves as a fluid set of requirements for an organization's project teams and is a tool that

teams can use to ensure that they only work on the most strategically viable or important items.

My recommended way forward for you is identical, but we're going to start your transformation on a much smaller scale. I would encourage you to conduct a "pilot" for your Agile Thinking transformation, which in non-industry terms simply means that we're going to start with one type of activity, improve it as best we can, and determine how best to apply the learnings to other parts of your life. We're going to frame out your pilot in the next few chapters and share some stories along the way. As we go forward, we're going to use Agile principles, some process improvement techniques, and other tidbits to drive improvements wherever they need to be driven.

All you need to do is take the leap. On three—ready? One... Two...

CHAPTER FOUR:

GETTING ALIGNED

...Three! Congratulations! By affirmatively deciding to take that leap, you just accomplished one of the hardest parts that any person or organization can achieve with an Agile Thinking transformation. Well done!

Getting aligned with your strategy to transition to Agile Thinking will need to happen in two stages:

- Understanding what you want to change about yourself to equip you to think in an Agile Thinking fashion; and
- Setting a path for yourself that will enable you to navigate the journey.

Alignment is an interesting concept within the corporate world. To get a transformation project to stick, the person or team doing the transformation needs to ensure that there is a clear consensus across *all* leaders in *all* affected parts of the company before that team kicks off the program. Typically, when I work with corporations on their organizational transformations, my first step is to subject all decision makers to an all-day (or half day, depending on the size and scope of the transformation) session where the focus is solely on aligning executives on the work that needs to be performed. My goal is as much political as it is transformational: I want to ensure that the *entire* team *generally* and *collectively* agrees on what we need to do together. This goes beyond just identifying which functions will be transformed and how the company's strategy will benefit from newfound efficiency, accountability, quality, and cost—the real reason is to make sure that no one can come back later and say, "This isn't what we agreed to do." Sneaky, but effective.

A successful outcome of the session is pretty straightforward, actually: let's all get together and achieve near total alignment on how the transformation will be done, who will do it, and how the company's functions will be performed to result in the best value for the company and its stakeholders. Easy, right?

No. But that's OK.

Total, internal *personal* alignment is your next step, as you are the primary stakeholder in this transformation. You won't need an entire day, but you will need to have a goal for yourself similar to what I described above. Think about the things you'd like to change in the way you live and work. Is it your personal efficiency? Is it an overall streamlining of your family budget or operating costs? Is it time management? If you've made it this far in the book, then my guess is that it's at least one of these items, or in some cases, all three.

Getting yourself aligned on how best to become an Agile Thinker is a personal journey for sure, but it isn't all that difficult if you consider the following dimensions:

1. Consider your own "organizational design." If you had a magic wand to change a part (or parts) of your life, what would the end result be? Would you be able to do things "smarter" and not "harder"? Do you want to become more accountable to yourself, your friends or family, or your work colleagues?

2. Know the "what" and the "how" of the areas you identified in question one. Confirm and validate how you do things today, paying particular attention to—and please excuse the corporate jargon here—the high-level process flows, the activities that are part of those flows, the inputs that precede them, and the outputs that result. As an example, if your area of focus is to find a better way of managing the routine that gets your kids out the door to the school bus every morning, lay out how you get them out today, what you have to do in order to shoo them off to school, and what happens once they actually land in a seat on the cheese wagon.

3. Break down and decompose the activities of your chosen area of improvement and learn how to define what goes into the activity (inputs) and what results from the activity (outputs). Using the school bus example above, this step will help you easily identify those parts of your morning routine that can be optimized so that you have more time (or preserve more of your sanity) in the mornings.

4. Now, find the "who." This is "who," with a small "w" (any requests to contact Roger Daltrey or Pete Townshend, while outside the scope of this writing, can most certainly be made through their publicists). When thinking of your "who," think about all of the people or roles that are required to perform each of the tasks that make up the activity you set out to improve. Then, map those roles to your desired vision of how your activity will improve, paying particular attention to those roles that may be inefficient along the way. If we're still school busing here, look at all of the people who are typically involved in your daily routine and try your best to identify the activities they need to perform in order to do their part. My third child (twelve years old at the time of writing) is a smart kid, but *always* loses his shoes—conveniently, just before he needs to meet the bus at the stop, 150 yards away. In order for him to find his shoes, an Agile Thinker would find a way to better empower him to find those kicks (probably by placing them near the door). Groans/rolled eyeballs/Captain Obvious reactions expected.

5. Finally, get aligned on your change and agree with yourself that it's a good idea. If you can't agree in your own mind, you will never be able to convince others that your proposed change is worth a flip.

Are you ready to start? Good! Even if you aren't ready to start, then this is also good! If you can bring yourself to get through the self-alignment portion of your transition to Agile Thinking, then now is the time to identify some "enablers" to help make the change actionable. I won't burden you with another list, but here is another list for you:

- Did you align with yourself? Have all behaviors required for the change been identified? Has a vision of what success looks like been drafted? If not, then it's back to the above list for you!
- If you did align, have you achieved clarity on what the vision for change is? Have you thought through the implications—both positive and negative—of making the required Agile Thinking changes? Again, if you've answered "no" to any of these questions, please get thyself back to the list above and think through your ideal state and how you think you would like to achieve it.
- Does everyone you interface with understand his or her role in the change, and do your affected stakeholders appreciate the impact of you making the change?
- Are you ready to rock?

If the answer to #4 above is a "yes," then turn your amp to eleven and follow me.[12]

---

12   Karen Murphy, Christopher Guest, Michael McKean, Harry Shearer, and Rob Reiner. *This is Spinal Tap*. Santa Monica, CA: Metro Goldwyn Mayer Home Entertainment. 1984.

If you're reading this and haven't seen the movie, get thyself over to Netflix and make it happen!

CHAPTER FIVE:

WHAT'S YOUR STORY?

———

If you're wondering if I actually just made an electric guitar noise just now, wonder no more. I totally did. I did it because I'm really excited about this next step we're going to take. This step involves stories, which for right-brained thinkers like me, are excellent ways to get points across.

Throughout history, stories have been an invaluable tool for explaining complex concepts more clearly, teaching the young, and instituting some semblance of order. In many cases a good story—like a picture—can be worth a thousand words.

The wonderful thing about Agile Thinking is that a good story is central to building your capability to rearrange, reprocess, and reprioritize your life. Stories are the core element of currency among organizations that practice Agile, so we'd be remiss if we didn't spend at least a few minutes reflecting on how a story can impact or improve your ability to manage your life.

In order to correctly explain the concept of how a story fits your life, we need to start the discussion with goals. We all have goals, whether it is to lose fifteen pounds (my current goal), learn to speak a foreign language, or develop a critical skill at work to improve job performance and enable that next promotion. All of these are straightforward examples, but you and I both know that each has several moving parts that will turn the goal into a reality. In order to really understand how you are going to get from where you are today to the point where the goal is realized, you'll need a list or roadmap that will help you get there. Losing weight can be realized by implementing a list of changes related to diet and exercise. Learning a language means taking a class, immersing yourself in a culture, or committing to ten minutes on Duolingo every day. You get the point.

Realizing goals can be an Agile Thinker's finest hour, and you will have the stories to prove it. Stories are the very elements that will help you lay out the way forward to meeting a goal. In Agile, "stories" are like very detailed items on a shopping list. They are loosely defined as a meaningful unit of work that can be completed by a team (or, in this case, an individual—you) within a defined period of time and, if satisfied, will end up with quantified, measurable results. Instead of the older way of thinking about tasks or projects where an organization would say, "This system shall do X, Y, and Z," they put the focus on what an end user would want in a way that is much easier to understand.

The format typically used is: "As a [certain type of end user], I need to [perform a certain type of function] so that I can [get a certain outcome]."

This was quite revolutionary, as it changed how people thought about planning projects and communicating the outcomes back to the people who need to be satisfied the most: end users, customers, or stakeholders. Stories also forced teams to begin thinking about delivering parts of projects in smaller batches that were always prioritized correctly, so that the teams delivering the project could confidently say that they were delivering the most valuable parts of the project with the dollars they were given.

This is a powerful thing! Imagine a world in which you could only focus on the most important things that set you sailing toward your personal or professional goals. You know, doing the right things rather than just doing things right. We can make this happen by giving you your own stories. Consider the following examples:

You want to install a home theater. You have a general idea of the layout that you would like, the types of components you want to have, and a directional understanding of the audiovisual output that you expect to get out of all of it. You want to watch *Top Gun* and actually feel the jets fly by, right? Right. So let's break this down together. Your first move as a planner would be to research TVs or projection screens. As a viewer, you would like to view movies on a screen that is appropriately sized for the room and delivers a clear picture, so that you can actually see the sweat on the pilots' faces as they engage in their dogfights. That's a story. Congratulations.

Breaking this down further, your refined understanding of this part of the project would encourage your Agile Thinking mind to dive a bit deeper. As a viewer, you would like to view movies on an eighty-two-inch 2160p 4K Smart TV with high definition resolution so that people in the back of the room will have a clear, comfortable watching experience. With this in mind, you can more clearly and accurately decide which TV you want, within all applicable technical specifications, and move on to the next item on your list. Your Agile Thinking brain continues to create other stories, just like this one, and you form a list of stories to begin crafting your home theater.

Here's another scenario for you to consider: let's say your mother-in-law wants you to build her a garden shed with one door and one window. You have no idea what this shed is supposed to look like, but have a general idea as to the main requirements: the shed needs a floor, some walls (guessing four), a roof (guessing one), one door, and one window. You'll also most likely need to add some outer covering to make it match her house's facade or external decor. Experienced Agile Thinkers would begin to start organizing their thoughts by creating six, high level groups that can be broken down into stories. There is one for the foundation, one for the walls, one for the roof, one for the door, and so on. Since common sense dictates that we should start from the bottom up, here is how an Agile Thinker would begin to break down the stories that form the basis for laying the foundation and, ultimately, the floor:

"As a visitor to the garden shed, I would like to walk on a level floor so that I can comfortably and safely store my wares and perform minor gardening tasks."

This is a great start, but you will have to go a bit deeper. In order to achieve the story above, a few things need to happen: you need to create a foundation by leveling the ground and laying the foundation blocks. Once that is done, you can continue to build the floor, construct the support beams, frame the shed, and then cover it with a roof and exterior, all the while soliciting feedback from your mother-in-law so that the two of you can make sure that her "she-shed" is done right the first time. As you continue to talk through what the shed needs to look like with her, you will find that a few things are happening: first, you will spend some quality time with your mother in-law that you will never get back. This is a bonus. Second, you'll be able to more clearly understand what is most important to her throughout all phases of the project. This way you are all but guaranteed to be working on what is most important to your end customer. It's all about those interactions with individuals that inspired the signers of the Agile Manifesto, right? Right.

These are two very basic, high-level examples of how Agile Thinkers can think in stories. The first example took a relatively simple idea (the idea of a home theater) and broke it down into smaller components, starting with the high-definition television set. This way of thinking allowed the home theater builder to expose a single element of a complex project and get a lot of detail around it without getting lost in the weeds. If that home theater builder was able to build similar stories around the sound system components, lighting, seating, and extras (you will need a popcorn machine in your home theater to *really* impress your friends), then the project becomes a lot easier to understand. If the stories are even halfway decent, then you will have a good, working understanding of the project that aligns directly with the needs and wants of your end users (read: you and your friends who want to watch *Top Gun*). This way of thinking in stories allows many different kinds of people—be they corporate project managers, software developers, or folks just like you and me—to define our work and prioritize it more effectively.

In the same vein, the garden shed example brought some definition to a critical step in a project that had a critical stakeholder. The builder's mother-in-law could use the first story to immediately see whether the project was going to her satisfaction. Assuming she was to be the visitor that wanted the level floor so that she could store her gear or perform minor gardening tasks, she would be able to inspect the project at its earliest stages to judge whether the floor would be big enough to store equipment or facilitate a work bench. She would be able to make decisions early enough in the project to affect the direction of the shed construction without having to encounter rework. The builder, under her supervision, would be focusing on only that which is most valuable at the time, which ensured maximum value and minimal rework (efficiency at its best, but most likely at the expense of the builder's patience).

Why did this way of thinking come about? The reason is simple: the old way of building requirements needed an overhaul; the older, more traditional ways of generating business requirements were difficult to define when the organization knew the least amount about the end product. Why would you try to define something that you can't see, touch, or use? Also, why would you continue to ask those users how to build their system or solve their problem when neither one of you knows how to build or solve yet? Stories allow you to involve the users—much like our shed hero did with her mother-in-law. They allow all of us to find optimal ways of breaking our work into smaller batches and perform our work in such a way that it is easier to deliver and is most compatible with the end user.

Early Agilists believed that a requirement should introduce new ways of thinking about building software products that would ultimately fall in the laps of the customers who used them. They should have enough detail to give a directional view of what needs to be delivered, but brief enough to quickly assemble, organize, and be subject to reprioritization at a moment's notice. What's more, they had to be able to give anyone without context or background on the project a better-than-average chance of understanding what the team is being asked to do. They understood that priorities shift over time (as they are wont to do), that teams should expect the unexpected, that it is easier to work in smaller increments, and that, above all, those who want the end product must be able to communicate with those who are building the end product.

We should all endeavor to view our work in the same light. Using Agile Thinking techniques will allow us to more clearly understand the main elements of a project, the expectations of those ultimately benefiting from the work being done, and the work required to bring it to completion. Additionally, Agile Thinkers can focus on the most important elements of a body of work and position themselves to adapt to changes as they come. Given the fact that change is one of the only constants in life outside of death and taxes, this is a huge advantage!

Now that we have an idea of what a story is and does, we need to know whether the stories we, as Agile Thinkers, are learning to create are any good. Unfortunately, a story is only as good as the critics say that it is (if you're a critic reading this book, please just nod silently and move on... and be kind!). As our Agile Thinking brains begin to develop the mental muscle memory around building our stories, we will need a mechanism to internally evaluate them. After all, we want to make sure that they are appropriately structured, sufficiently clear, and easy to place and move on a priority list.

A 2003 article by Bill Wake, a recognized expert in coaching teams on Agile software development, gave us one of the best and most relatable models of story evaluation yet: the INVEST model.[13] Many times, our customers will describe their needs or wants, which will drive our story building. This requires us as Agile Thinkers to vet our own stories and determine whether they capture what they need to capture. INVEST (Independent, Negotiable, Valuable, Estimable, Small, and Testable) will help us to evaluate the quality of any story. If the story fails to meet any one of the criteria in the acronym, then it needs to be rewritten or discarded. Wake simply says that a good story must be:

---

13   Bill Wake, "INVEST in Good Stories, and SMART Tasks," *XP123: Exploring Extreme Programming* (blog), Accessed July 28, 2020.

- **Independent**—Each story must be an independent, incremental need, like a television or level foundation for a garden shed.

- **Negotiable**—Each story needs to give the doer of the project and the receiver or user of the project the ability to communicate openly about what is being delivered. We already established that change happens *all* the time, so having a mechanism to deal with that change and apply it to work being done on a project is paramount. No one wants to spend a lot of time trying to ensure that a story has every last detail. What happens when circumstances change tomorrow? I'll tell you: at a minimum, you're rewriting the story, and that is SO Waterfall!

- **Valuable**—Your stories will represent small bits of incremental value for your end users, customers, stakeholders, or you! Each story, when implemented, will give everyone the ability to constantly evaluate what is being delivered and will give all present the opportunity to provide and react to feedback. There are lots of great avenues for communication here, even with your mother-in-law.

- **Estimable**—If you can't quickly determine how much effort or cost is involved with accomplishing your story, then it may be way too dang big. Go back, rethink, and break it into smaller chunks if you can.

- **Small**—Speaking of small chunks, think of a story as something that should take you or your team a single day to deliver. This will allow you to show progress against the project or goal more easily and will keep you sane in the process.

- **Testable**—If you can't test your story in some way, shape, or form, then you will never know when it's complete. Tests can be the best ways to get to the root of stories—in fact, many Agile organizations involve testers early in story creation to make sure that this piece of INVEST holds up. If you can't let your mother-in-law see the size of the foundation or level the floor, then you won't be entirely confident that she will accept the finished product, can you?

If you've never been exposed to Agile, this way of thinking is a departure from what you may have been taught. Please know that other Agile Thinkers will identify with your growing pains, as we all went through the same transition.

We're all in this together, so to get you started on your story-making journey, I will add the following perspective as food for thought:

Your stories are conversation pieces. Think of a story as a commitment to having a later conversation—either with yourself (stop laughing, it's healthy) or with others—to complete a task. In the examples above, each project required some work with differing levels of complexity. Instead of spending hours upon hours researching TV specs, talking with pundits at home improvement stores, or listening to an in-law drone on and on about the curtains she wants in her gardening shed, our heroes kept it simple. They gained understanding for how they wanted to complete their respective projects using plain language that had just enough detail to get their projects started. The real value comes in discussing those stories with others as you progress along your project's path. The focus is not on the language itself per se, but on the outcome that results from it. To be successful as an Agile Thinker you will have to use your stories as a means of constant communication and negotiation with those involved with your project or goal. That way, all parties involved can be constant, vital parts of the story's completion, and all can be satisfied with its outcome.

As an Agile Thinker, I want to ensure that all reading this book try to create one to two stories and validate with the INVEST model, so that you can become familiar with the structure, form, and function (and successfully move on to the next chapter).

CHAPTER SIX

MASTERING SPACE AND TIME USING BACKLOGS

If you're not an expert on creating and validating stories yet, fear not! We have a few more items at our disposal that will help get you where you need to go on your Agile Thinking journey. Our next core concept is that of the *backlog,* or list, that will contain those stories. Now that we've spent a bit of time on what a story is and does, I think it's high time that we focus on the list that will contain those items.

Folks, meet Backlog. Backlog, meet everyone.

Now that the ice has been broken and pleasantries exchanged all around, we need to take a deeper dive into what a backlog is, why it is used, and how it can help us organize our lives to become more efficient, effective Agile Thinkers.

According to Kenneth Rubin's book *Essential Scrum,* the standard definition of a backlog is "a prioritized list of desired functionality. It provides a centralized and shared understanding of what to build and the order in which to build it. It is a highly visible artifact at the heart of Scrum [read: Agile—Scrum is a framework that software developers typically use to address problems and deliver value] that is accessible to all participants."[14]

In other words, it's a fancy list that, if used correctly, can provide clear visibility into what needs to be accomplished, how much effort or cost it will take to accomplish, and the order in which only those items that are important enough to make the cut are accomplished or achieved. It's more than milk, eggs, and butter at the grocery store, and it is certainly not the rear piece of wood in the fireplace; it is a powerful tool that helps people and teams become more effective in their delivery. In industry, any time there is a product or project being built, enhanced, or supported, there a backlog shall be. Backlogs contain items, ranked in order of importance or value, that will provide value to the end user or customer.

Provided your newly minted stories pass the INVEST sniff test (from the Bill Wake article we outlined in the previous chapter), we can begin to experiment with getting those stories ranked in order of importance with enough information in it to allow anyone to tell how much time each item will take. If we can do this successfully in this chapter, you will be off to the races with a new level of Agile Thinking.

---

14   Kenneth S. Rubin, *Essential Scrum: A Practical Guide to the Most Popular Agile Process* (Upper Saddle River, NJ: Pearson Education, Inc., 2012); Scrum Alliance, Inc. "Overview: What is Scrum?" Accessed July 21, 2020.

It should go without saying that a good Backlog will have the items that are most important to us or that we plan on working on soon ranked high on the list. They should be relatively small in size (now that we're thinking and planning in smaller batches) and have enough detail to allow us to estimate with confidence how long each item will take. The larger items, or those items that need to be done later or require further thought, should be toward the bottom of the list.

I know you must be asking yourself, "Well, Jeez, Jack—this can't be the only thing you're trying to teach us here. We've been successfully making lists for years! How is this new material?" The answer, my Agile Thinking friends, is all about "The End."

"The End" is my term for an imaginary line that exists in all backlogs. One of the most advantageous aspects of Agile is that the delivery date for a project always stays static; the budget may change, the stuff being produced may change, but the due date and core team personnel do not. This allows for a greater sense of predictability and transparency into team composition and costs, and it establishes a hard stop, typically expressed as an end date, within which a team must complete its work. You see, a project is just like real life: when you start out with a project you know the bare minimum about how the project will end. It is through communication, negotiation, and estimation that we learn more about what it is we are trying to do, and just like the best of all laid plans, they are subject to change at a moment's notice. Sound familiar? How many times have you set out to do something only to have life get in the way? Thousands, I'm guessing.

"The End," also referred to in my professional circles as "The Line of Death," the "Edge of Tomorrow," or more professionally, the team's "Long-Term Capacity." Whatever you would like to call it, it is a limit that allows—nay, forces—you or someone you're working with to consistently choose only the most important items to focus on. To illustrate, let's take ourselves back to our gardening shed example we looked at earlier. For the sake of discussion, let's imagine that the builder's mother-in-law had a hard deadline of six days from her initial ask to complete the shed (she's hosting the Garden Club Party at her home and really wants to one-up the rest of the members). The deadline she sets for six days from now is what I would call The End in that builder's backlog. If every item added to the garden shed backlog was adequately detailed and estimated, the builder would have a very clear idea as to not only how long each item takes, but more importantly how many items will actually get done in a six-day period. If the sum of all of the items in her backlog carry her project past The End, then she needs to have a very meaningful conversation with her mother-in-law to determine which items, if any, need to be dropped from her feature list. I'm guessing that the level floor, walls, and roof have to stay on the Backlog, as they are critical to the shed's construction. But the circular window? The curtains? These are items that, through meaningful conversation, may be able to fall off of the list so that the builder can focus on only the most important or valuable items.

This concept is critical to Agile Thinking. You can establish a hard and fast due date for yourself, your project team, or a goal, and have a very powerful mechanism to ensure that you're only focusing on the most valuable or strategically important items. The backlog can reduce waste in the form of wasted time, working on the wrong stuff, or misinterpretations of priorities and ensure that the project or progress toward achieving your goal is kept aligned and on track. This is why this chapter implies that you can "master space and time" by using a backlog. With a fixed due date, you are in complete control of your delivery time frame—nothing slips! The items you need to accomplish from today to your due date is the space within which you have to work. Mastering this concept will allow you to master both.

CHAPTER SEVEN:

OUR NEW NORMAL: MANAGING BACKLOGS AMIDST A PANDEMIC, AND OTHER CHEERFUL TOPICS

Introducing the concept of managing backlogs is difficult to understand for many. If you are one of those people, then fear not: the universe has provided us all with a fascinating view of how to utilize them in real life. As I write this, we are at a point of global uncertainty that neither my generation nor my parents' generation had to experience.

Pandemics are interesting. Scary, but interesting. Throughout history, they have played a major role in shaping the development (or regression) of global civilizations and have allowed for renewed focus on how we live, how we work, and how we maintain standards of hygiene. Take the "Black Death," for example: the Black Death (or, Bubonic Plague, caused by the bacterium *Yersinia pestis)*, killed 30 to 40 percent of the European population from the 1340s to 1400, and it kept recurring often until the late 1700s.[15]

One of the most interesting things about what happened during the Black Plague was not how the pandemic spread, but rather across the ways of how the pandemic was stopped. People back then became intimately aware that keeping their hands clean was linked to better hygiene and, transitively, a better chance of survival. This is interesting because this is yet another example of how humanity innovates through times of great hardship and tragedy. We are an adaptable system: we change, and we overcome, just as we are learning to do in the face of the current COVID-19 (or, "Coronavirus," or, if you're southern like me, "with all this going on") crisis. As a global society, we are learning to work in directions that we didn't navigate before. We wear yoga pants to work and quite often don't shave or shower before meetings. I went an entire work week without wearing shoes. It's different, for sure, and not necessarily in a bad way.

Borrowing the scary old consulting adage, "in chaos, there is opportunity," I tried to look at the pandemic as an opportunity to help refine our newly-minted Agile Thinker brains and focused on the brightest of the bright sides: the elimination of the commute. Like it or not, losing our commutes has really forced us to live and work in an alternative method. Before COVID-19, we would get up, get to work, execute a

---

15   World Health Organization, "Plague Fact Sheet," Last modified October 2017.

bunch of tasks, and come home, only to repeat the process the next day. We managed our lives via two distinct backlogs: the one for work, and the one that we needed to pick up the moment we returned home. Our daily routines centered around managing one backlog, celebrating successes or bemoaning failures, taking a trip home, and then working on the home front, only to have to celebrate or bemoan productivity in the house.

This was our collective life before March 2020.

During the pandemic, though, that dynamic changed radically. We became accustomed to a "new normal" that forced our work backlogs to merge with our personal backlogs. Worlds collided. Conference calls became the norm, we utilized video services with WebEx and Zoom, and we learned to work productively at home. It was no longer gauche to attend a call with executives while feeding a baby, or to have a dog barking in the background. Our personal lives became our professional lives, and vice versa. For some people, your author included, the measure of productivity changed. Before COVID, I measured productivity by looking at the velocity that I was able to achieve for myself at work, reflected on it (a "personal retrospective," if you will), and then did the same when my work at home ceased later that night. Remember velocity from Chapter Two? Essentially, velocity is the measure of what a team can produce in a specific amount of time. For most of us in the world of project management and software development, velocity is a method for accurately measuring the rate at which a Scrum team delivers "business value." When that specified amount of time completes, the team should be able to add up all of the effort (normally expressed in "points," but for our purposes as practically living adults we'll stick with hours) for the items they finished or delivered. The aggregated number of points (or, hours for us) associated with the stories they completed during the block of time is the team's velocity.

In our case, we typically work with a constant stream of incoming tasks, so a good way to measure our velocity is to count the number of tasks marked as done in a single day. If you average these daily velocities over the course of a week, you can begin to estimate how much work you would be able to get through in a longer time (like a week or a month, if your life circumstances drive you to look out that far on your tasks lists). Knowing your velocity is important, because you will begin to think, recognize, and constantly revise the estimate of how long your projects will take to complete. This ability to predict task duration will serve you well and will definitely become more accurate over time.

Which is what became very interesting during the initial stages of the pandemic: we as a society were forced to combine our two sets of backlogs and work them together. Gone were the commutes that broke up the activities between our personal and professional lives. We began to think not of the dual task lists, but of the single, integrated backlog that forced us to identify those items that were most important at that time. To borrow the phrase from former Notre Dame head football coach Lou Holtz, we began to integrate our lives by focusing on "what's important now." We started to guide ourselves and our choices by taking the backlog items that needed addressing first and then measuring the impact or outcomes of each, regardless of the level of gratification that a completed task gave us in the past.[16] Our important "business value" came from those items that we were able to complete and had the most positive impact on our lives, and we became able to prioritize both our personal and professional decisions, choices, and actions.

This is equivalent to hand washing during the Black Plague! We were forced to innovate in the face of a terrible situation and ultimately gave ourselves a way to become more productive. From our *couches*. Now, let's get one thing clear: I am not making an argument for a more permanent go-forward work from home arrangement for the lot of us. In fact, I am a big believer in getting things done in person, and due to age or social bias I don't intend to deviate from that belief any time soon. What I believe we can all learn from this is how to focus on what is important—today and in the future—by using Agile Thinking techniques such as integrating our backlogs. Consider the following example from my world: I have a son, who we will refer to as "Henry," due in large part to the fact that his name is actually "Henry." Henry is in junior high and, like just about every other student across the modern world during this pandemic, is involved in the new and lightly tested concept of studying and learning at home known as "e-learning," Henry is a person who needs structure in his academic life, as he is a highly creative, right-brained person; if his imagination or creativity gets the best of him, all other areas of focus are immediately put at risk. With obligations that are normally associated with learning

---

16   Lou Holtz, *Winning Every Day: The Game Plan for Success*, (New York: Harper Business, 1998).

Also, Go Irish!

in a classroom setting now in the home, it was hard for him to prioritize his school tasks and those tasks normally associated with the area of his life where he spends his leisure time. No knock on Henry—these were things that we all had to deal with during the pandemic of 2020. Pretty standard.

What we found with Henry is not that he needs the structure just for structure's sake; rather, he needed a way to visualize the importance of each outcome by using stories. As we saw back in Chapter Five, stories (if done correctly) can be extraordinarily valuable. A good story can be central to building your capability to rearrange, reprocess, and reprioritize your life, which is what we needed the most when our two worlds collided.

We knew we were in trouble with Henry when we got an email from three of his teachers saying that he hadn't turned in any of his assignments in weeks. No bueno. Against our better judgement, we decided not to yell at Henry, but rather dig deeper into what was influencing his choices. My spouse and I came from a world where if you didn't get your assignments done in time—and I mean, every time—your ability as a seventh grader to get into Princeton or Stanford or whichever college your parents wanted you to attend diminished rapidly. When we sat with Henry and talked through the situation, he was crushed. He was getting the work done on his iPad, but never turned the work in the afternoons due to the fact that he had a standing task—assigned by us, I might add—to begin household chores. Two worlds, two backlogs, one cataclysmic collision.

We needed to start simply with Henry so that we could avoid the impact of two backlogs colliding. Using our story format, we questioned him about what his teachers expected of their students. In Agile Thinking parlance, we asked, "As a math teacher, what do I expect Henry to do to get credit for an assignment so that he can get a passing grade?"

His answer was just as simple: "As a student, I need to turn in my math assignment so that I can play Fortnite."

Not exactly what his parents wanted to hear, but it was a start. Small victories are victories indeed—they're just celebrated a bit differently.

We pulled the thread further by introducing velocity. We talked about homework being a table stakes expectation from a teacher. They expect the students to complete their work in the span of a day, and it shall be ever thus. Few parents will disagree with that. In other words, the stack of homework Henry receives virtually becomes a part of his daily backlog for delivery. Both his parents and teachers alike agree: you need to get your work done on time so that your grades can stay buoyant and your parents can stay sane. And play Fortnite, I guess.

Now, the added complexity of the home life: we asked Henry about his obligations at home. Henry, as a junior high student, needs to be able to do his own laundry, clean the kitchen once per day, and make sure that the dog goes out in the morning. These three things can be added to his backlog so that the most important item on the list (the dog) gets done in the morning so that our carpets can stay intact. Then, Henry can sequence through his homework backlog until he reaches a point where he can clean the kitchen, have some time to play his video games, and schedule a laundry session or two once a week. He didn't know it, but we gave him a different mode of operations: though he missed the structure that he was missing from his classroom setting, he was getting another form—one that he can control—through the concept of a personal backlog. We'll make an Agile Thinker out of him if it kills us.

The epilogue to all of this is that Henry began to view his life through the lens of someone who is managing a fluid list. He wanted to make sure that his completion rate of stories (his velocity) was steady for his schoolwork and increasing by week so that he could have more time to play his video games. He found a good balance in his workload so that he always focused on the most important tasks at the right time without spending too much time and effort on tasks that either don't matter or aren't of value. In other words, he was completing what needed to be done while opening more time to do what he wanted to do. This is the basis of Agile Thinking, and it was learned by a seventh grader.

His parents' next move was to buy him a bike, because:

"As a parent I want my child to go outside so that he doesn't spend every waking hour on video games."

Get outside, Henry.

CHAPTER EIGHT:

CONNECTING THE DOTS: MANAGING YOUR FLOW AS AN AGILE THINKER

———

So we've covered some heady stuff so far: we've dipped our Agile Thinking toes into managing WIP, creating stories, using Kanban boards, and crafting backlogs. This is a lot to process, and we're going to discuss how to bring these all together now. In the next section, I will lay out some practical examples for you based on my personal and professional life experience that will illustrate the concepts that we explored together here.

The minute you put this book down, you will have a decent feel for what I would consider to be the Agile Thinking "basics": those elements from Agile software development and continuous improvement that you can apply to your own personal life to make you more efficient and effective.

My first year as a young junior officer in the United States Navy was focused on attaining my Surface Warfare pin, or my "water wings," as the vernacular goes. The pin is similar in concept to the golden wings that military pilots earn when they are qualified to fly their aircraft. The pin says that you are able to drive, navigate, and even deploy the ship's weapons, and it represents a milestone in the career of every officer in the surface navy. When I earned mine, I stood proudly in front of my commanding officer—who, I might add, did not make it easy to earn—eagerly waiting for him to pin it on me. When it became my time, he briefly congratulated me and then reminded me that passing all of the tests was not the crowning achievement that I thought it was but a mere statement that I met the minimum requirements to drive his ship.

It simply meant that today I knew the least about how to drive the ship. I was crushed at first, but quickly saw the wisdom in his words, and over time I began to put my skills, my career, and even the ways in which I did things in perspective. While my message to you isn't as harsh, the logic still holds: if you take one or all of these tools with you into your lives, then congratulations—you just took the first step in your thousand-mile journey. Instead of deflating (like I did briefly when I heard the captain say what he did about my minimum level of competence), think of this as your finest hour!

A quick review of what we have learned together so far will bring this all into perspective:

- You, as a newly minted (read: self-proclaimed) Agile Thinker can now understand and determine your WIP limits;

- You, as an Agile Thinker, can now determine new ways to organize your thoughts around complex tasks using stories;
- You, as an Agile Thinker, can organize those stories in a backlog that will ensure you will always work on those tasks that bring you the most value to your project, goal, or life; and
- You, like me, can use these tools to begin to improve any aspect of your personal or professional life.

Not too shabby for beginners like us, right? Right. These items above are based on very, very basic but proven Agile concepts that have been tested in the industry. We will review these together quickly here now, as a refresher, and in the next section I will show you some practical, real-life examples of how the techniques can be applied in practice.

As we started to reflect on why Agile came about in the first place, several things became clear: first, the world was at a place where new ways of doing things needed to become reality; second, that which worked yesterday is not necessarily a good fit for today; and third, humans need to constantly reinvent the ways in which they communicate and interact, especially given the pace of change, access to technology, and our ever-increasing need to consume information.

The key to tying all of these tools together is your flow. "Flow," by a loose enterprise definition, is how enterprises become more adaptive and agile in delivering work effectively.[17] It

---

17 Lean Enterprise Institute, Inc., "Knowledge Center: Flow," Lean Institute Knowledge Center, Accessed July 21, 2020.

means the enterprise is essentially making decisions on delivered work based on an iterative understanding of the needs of their markets, changing customer needs, and their own internal delivery mechanisms. In essence, flow is about greater business agility (i.e. finding ways to do things better, faster, and more efficiently) and delivering value (or, focusing on only those things that are the most important at that time for the company).

Sound familiar? It should. Flow hits at the core of what we have been talking about all throughout this book: that there are better ways of doing things in our personal and professional lives, and that we, as Agile Thinkers, are going to find them. Flow is a way to take all of the concepts discussed here and wrap them up into a container that will help guide our Agile thoughts.

Consider the backlog that we discussed earlier. As you know, a backlog is more than just a fancy list: it is a crucial tool that will allow you, the Agile Thinker, to get faster at identifying those stories that are important to you and become more purposeful in how you prioritize your daily activities. The backlog allows us to "deliver value" in our daily lives, right in the face of the uncertainty that our daily lives throw at us on a regular and ongoing basis. Paying proper attention to your backlog will allow you to live in a constant state of planning and doing, and it will ensure that you're focused on what's really important in life. You will constantly be shifting your priorities based on the curveballs that life throws at you, and you will always think in terms of what you must do to achieve your goals and avoid work that is wasteful.

Agile Thinkers will always keep a good balance between items coming into their backlogs and items that they are completing. In fact, the backlog is a good check to see if our planning and doing is moving at an optimal pace. If we are lazy in our ability to think through stories, then the volume of work coming into the backlog will slow. If that arrival rate of new stories gets too slow, then the backlog will run dry and we go right back to where we were before we started Agile Thinking. On the other hand, too many stories hitting your backlog at once will cause a lot of wasted thinking on priorities, plans, and other aspects of life that we don't need to engage in at the moment. As with everything, moderation and balance are key. If you're getting too many items on your list, walk away, go do yoga, and come back to it later! This is a great time to flex your new WIP reducing muscles that we initially developed in Chapter Two.

My recommendation is that you only include enough items on your list for the next two to three weeks of activity. This will always depend on how big the undertaking you're setting out to do is, but as a general rule, it tends to hold up. Besides the fact that you are a forward-thinking individual and over-all great human being, the reason why you should have a few weeks' worth of items is your velocity. The velocity, or the speed at which you achieve completion of backlog items, should get faster over time. When you create your initial backlog and try to populate it with your first batch of stories, you will stumble. It's most likely going to be a total departure from where you think today, so steel yourself and deal with it. Failure is a big part of Agile Thinking, as failure enables us to learn our limits, identify our inefficiencies, and incorporate some serious learning! To date, not one of the teams I have trained in industry-standard Agile got things right in their first three iterations, and all of them were able to get better over time. You will be no different. Just keep in mind that if you want to think in an Agile fashion, you need to be Agile.

Use these new tools to connect what you have learned and accelerate good results, and you'll see your productivity begin to spike.

Let's take a look at another real-world, practical example: My friend Mike is a very accomplished Agile Coach and leader of Chicago's Agile Professional Learning Network (aplnchicago. org). Mike doesn't just *do* Agile; he *is* Agile. He is an Agile Thinker in every sense of the word, and to illustrate the kind of street cred he's carrying, I'd like to give you an example of how true Agile Thinkers like Mike can organize, prioritize, and effectively execute large projects.

Mike and his lovely wife Becky live in a single-family home in the northwest suburbs of Chicago. Their house of nineteen years has been a happy place for their family; it's where they raised their kids and threw absolutely legendary Halloween parties. It was a great environment, until they ran into a problem: excessive moisture in their already finished basement.

Quick aside: if you've never lived in the Midwest, the finished basement is an important part of living in this area of the country. To us, the basement is more than just a domain or "person cave;" it is a place to seek shelter in times of rough weather, it insulates us from the brutal Midwestern winters, and it is a place to watch your team not make the Super Bowl every year (I'm looking at you, fellow Bears fans). Long story short, our basements are a huge part of our lives.

The dilemma that Mike and Becky faced is a common one with finished basements. Finding moisture in an area of the house that is underground happens from time to time, and when it does, action needs to be taken immediately. If you're not careful, moisture can lead to mold in your carpets, behind your walls, and even in drop ceiling tiles. Bad news. Since Mike and Becky are people of education and discipline, they naturally took a "scorched earth" approach to cleaning: everything had to be gutted, down to the studs, lest they, their family, and potential guests at Halloween time become subject to myriad health issues.

The issue they faced was not determining what actually needed to be done; rather, it was where to start. Mike and Becky are practical, handy people, and they each had their own idea as to where the project needed to start once the demolition was complete. They ripped everything out of the basement, again down to the studs, and spent a significant amount of time fixing leaks and dehumidifying the space. They purchased some supplies, such as new wall board, and had other supplies all over the house. They felt as if they were in a decent position to start the project and they both had a general idea of the things that needed to be done; they just didn't anticipate the difficult conversation(s) around the most contentious, most important part: where to start.

Quick aside, number two: each person's commitment to the project was also deeply rooted in their commitment to each other, as once you've been married for a while, each partner knows when to act, or more importantly, when not to act; when to talk, or more importantly, when not to talk. You get the picture.

Becky felt that the first step in the new basement was to paint the floor with a vapor proof paint. Mike didn't disagree that the floor needed repainting, but felt that painting the floor was not necessarily the first place to start. They, like any good married couple or strong partnership, knew that in order to be successful on this project, they needed to align. As the old proverb goes, "a journey of a thousand miles begins with a single step," and their thousand-mile journey began with the step of understanding what step one was. Becky wanted the floor painted first so that the couple could have a tangible sign of progress. In her words, "If we paint the floor, then we will have accomplished something." Any one of us could easily agree with Becky and get the project underway, but Mike could think of several activities that had to happen before the floor could be painted, and they would definitely take more than a weekend to complete that part of the project. Like any good Agile Thinker, he armed himself with multiple colors of sticky notes, a Sharpie, and some poster board and began to build stories. Mike knows that Becky is a visual thinker, so he went for maximum impact (by the by, Trello wasn't available at the time).

If you're ever in a position similar to the one in which Mike and Becky found themselves, a good tool for you to use is to start with a conversation. Grab a Trello board, some sticky notes, or even a flip chart or legal pad, and begin talking with your project team. Mike's approach was to begin identifying those items—their stories—that would make up their remodel. Their initial list of potential stories looked something like this:

- Finish walls—to finish the walls, we need insulation to keep us warm, wall board to make it look nice, and other items.
- Drop ceiling—once the walls are complete, we need to put in a new drop ceiling architecture to accommodate a new lighting configuration to allow for new features in the basement.
- New features—new features, you say? What if we had a gaming area in one part of our basement or a bar that would allow us to have people over for entertaining?
- Lighting—we talked about the drop ceiling, so let's look at new lights to support the new feature category we just created above.
- Electrical—if we have new lighting, we will have to re-run the electrical to accommodate new switches. This totally makes sense.
- The floor—we will need to clear out everything, repair any cracks, use the vapor barrier paint per Becky's initial direction, and decide on a padding and ultimate floor-covering option.

Mike and Becky had each category identified on a board in their house and even had dependencies (typically, those items that need to be completed before something else can start or finish) identified. They devoted each weekend—their sprint cadence—to begin work and their initial agreement on velocity was initially defined as the amount of work they could get done during the course of a weekend. They were primed to execute just as we are learning to do together. The project—and the marriage—seemed to have a plan with all risks of failure successfully mitigated. Great news.

Their sprints started out awkwardly, as they tend to do with any new project. After one weekend, they realized that they were able to actually get some things done but overcommitted in some areas. Totally normal behavior for new Agile projects, but after that first Sunday night, Mike came into his kitchen to find Becky staring at their board with a dejected look on her face.

"What's wrong?" he said.

"We didn't accomplish anything," she replied.

"Why do you feel that way? Of course we accomplished some things—look at the sticky notes that we moved from the 'To-Do' column over to the 'Done' column. That, my dear, is both progress *and* accomplishment."

Becky's reply shocked Mike: "Well, we didn't get to paint the floor."

Because Mike is a good husband and life partner, he was able to see the world from her point of view, and realized their first mistake: in their zeal to organize and align on the big picture, they never tied off and committed to an agreed-upon first step. The processes were in place (using a Kanban board for organization, dependencies were identified and managed), the tools were in place (the stories, the velocity), but the interactions with the individuals were not as strong as they should have been.

"We didn't actually pull the floor painting task into this sprint," Mike said quietly.

"I know. But I figured we would just finish all the stuff we said we'd do, and maybe pull that one in early. But we didn't even finish all the things we thought we'd do this weekend!"

At that last statement, Mike had to admit that Becky was completely justified in being upset about what they hadn't finished, just maybe not about the floor painting. The number of dependent tasks that preceded the floor painting were laid out on the board. Painting the floor was many *weeks* away. But she definitely had a point about their progress, and Mike knew it.

His role as an Agile Thinker was to take a step back and reflect with Becky on why they didn't get as much done as expected. In retrospect, the answer was obvious. Renovating the basement was not a full-time job for either of them; they still had a house to run. There was the time spent mowing the yard, doing the laundry, or taking their daughter to work. All that day-to-day maintenance was still out there. They needed to adjust their own expectations by taking some of that mundane work into account. He had a plan.

His plan, like so many other Agile Thinker plans, had to start simple. Mike began to identify other areas of their day-to-day operations inside of their house that required work. He created a story category for things like yard work, for laundry, for other home maintenance, which shifted the focus not just on the large basement project, but on all of the other activities that shifted the focus or attention away from the basement project. In essence, he was able to map out their entire weekend lives on a Kanban board just as we have been discussing all throughout this book. He even went so far as to create an Excel spreadsheet that showed the progress made each weekend and tied directly to those stories that were listed in the "Done" column so that each spouse could track what was done, what was still yet to be accomplished, and how their weekend lives were impacting their ability to track toward their goal. It worked. By the end of the exercise they were able to increase their household flow—their own agility—across multiple tracks of work, and they still use it to manage large household projects today.

The best part? Becky moved her floor painting story to "Done" the day they completed that part of the job. And yes, they accomplished something—as Agile Thinkers, as new finished basement owners, and as a couple.

SECTION THREE:

THE STORIES

I am a right-brained, non-linear thinker. It was absolute hell in college calculus and in engineering graduate school, but life is a series of choices, so I dealt with it.

Because I use the right side of my brain, I am a visual learner. I believe a picture is worth a thousand words and appreciate new ways to help learners like me get the point.

Before you scream at me to actually get to the point, or before you throw out the old joke about my left brain not having anything right in it and my right brain not having anything left in it, I'd like to submit some stories to help tie the concepts we've been learning together... well, together.

Stories have long been used as a way to explain the unexplainable or to simply articulate a point. Parables in scripture texts and even cave paintings or detailed inscription on Gaelic crosses served as valuable tools to explain new concepts to people and serve as a lasting record for future generations.

This book contains none of that.

Kidding aside, if someone tells his or her kids that they are using a book on Agile to plan for a vacation or get people out of the door more quickly in the morning, then I will consider that a win.

The stories in this section are true and are based on actual experience. They serve to inform, entertain, or show you what not to do. Treat them as good, illustrative examples on how you can apply these principles to your daily lives, and we'll call it good.

We'll meet a law firm that decided to adopt Agile, despite not being in the business of developing software at all; a major drywall and building materials company that wanted to get its products to market more quickly and with fewer errors; and finally, a bit from yours truly on how I used Agile to write this book.

If you elect to adopt Agile Thinking into your life, you will no doubt have stories of your own, but for now you're stuck with mine. Happy reading!

CHAPTER NINE:

LAWYERS CAN BE AGILISTS TOO!

———

My readers who practice law will need to forgive me for what I am about to say: I find the entire legal industry to be very boring. I mean, I will never pretend to understand the ins and outs of what it takes to be a lawyer, including and especially that first, very special year of law school. Since I have a long-standing policy of always admitting when I am wrong or in need of help, I will be the first person to admit when I need to seek counsel from an attorney. It's that simple. Well, that and the fact that I married one, which usually means that I am in some need of an attorney pretty much all of the time.

During my consulting career, I worked with several large, technologically-driven companies to transform their mode of operations from an older model of software delivery to Agile. This is a very complex exercise for all involved—me, the consultant, and all parts of the affected enterprise, to be sure. By far, the hardest part of any Agile transformation is exactly what the name implies—transforming a large group of people who are most likely resistant to change over to a new way of doing things that they know nothing about. Fear, uncertainty, doubt, and other "organizational antibodies" can directly affect the success or failure of a transformation, which means that in order to ensure adoption—that is, the organization's willingness and ability to make that change stick—the transformer(s) need(s) to make sure that the organization is united under a common purpose. I was fortunate in the transformations that I led because most, if not all, were all in need of a faster and more effective way to get their technology products to market.

So when a large, suburban law firm outside of Chicago called me for help, I was a bit hesitant to take that first meeting. Why on earth would a law firm—those stereotypically stodgy, white-shoe groups of well-paid individuals who practice the dark arts of the legal field—need Agile? Do they need a faster way to put their client-facing documents together? Do they need to be faster at producing those personal injury or meso-thelioma commercials than the next group? What could they possibly want with me?

The answer was in large part my inspiration for this book. As I met with them, I determined that their backlog of work (the amount of work they had in their To-Do bin) was, apparently, entirely too large for the cadre of attorneys that they employed to service it. Their books of business were driving so much work into their associates and partners that they were having trouble keeping up with it all. They were, as the saying goes, becoming victims of their own success: they were on an unsustainable path that would ultimately lead to, at best, employee burnout and, at worst, legal exposure for a missed detail or malpractice claim.

When you take on a strategically-significant consulting project in any organization, the first step is to do some serious discovery or all of the fact-finding you can do to determine the underlying problems the organization is facing. After all, I would hate to make a recommendation not based entirely on fact or, worse, based on faulty analysis.

Conducting a detailed review of this law firm seemed easy enough as they had about a thousandth of the employees of my last transformation client. Should be easy, right?

Actually, no. It was way more complex than I thought it would be. This group had a massive issue with its queueing system. In other words, the number of items that arrive on your To-Do list needs to have a good balance with the rate of completion. This is what allows the owner of the To-Do list to add more items and to feel the dopamine commonly associated with completing items on a list (look that one up—it's true).[18] For this group, the arrival rate of legal work became out of sync with the team's ability to complete that work. If you want to think of this in mathematical terms, you can think of the arrival as the rate of items showing up in their case coffers per unit of time:

Arrival Rate = (1 item) / (Unit of time)[19]

---

18 E.J. Masicampo and R.F. Baumeister, "Consider It Done! Plan Making Can Eliminate the Cognitive Effects of Unfulfilled Goals." *Journal of Personality and Social Psychology* 101, (June 2011): 667-683.

19 Kenneth Chelst, and Tom Edwards, "Queuing Systems and Formula," High School Operations Research (HSOR), accessed July 21, 2020.

So in this case, if a new legal case arrived on the doorstep of this law firm every hour (sixty minutes), the arrival rate is not sixty, but one per sixty. The lead time, or the average amount of time that piece of legal work sits waiting to be accomplished, will also need to be expressed as a unit of time, hopefully commensurate with the time units for the arrival rate. So if one case comes in every sixty minutes, we needed to measure the amount of time—in minutes—that case sat idle before being addressed and completed. This firm needed to understand how to best create flow by getting to the core of measuring the following:

Number of cases waiting to be addressed = (the rate cases enter and leave the system) x (the average amount of time the cases spend in process)

In order to get to the bottom of their problem, we needed to put our WIP-reducing caps on (after laying out our WIP yoga mats!) and reduce the amount of time that the cases were spending in their process system. We'll call this "W." Reducing W means that we will have clear visibility into whether the team will be successful in completing the work and reducing risk to the firm. So, if we want to figure out the total picture of how this firm is currently managing itself, we can use the equation $W=L/A$, where again, W equals the time to process all of their items in queue, L equals the number of items inside the queueing system, and A is our arrival rate. In a subgroup of six attorneys, they currently had over forty-eight active cases waiting to be administered, a business development arm that averaged two new cases per day, and had a standard turnaround time of two weeks per case.

Let's run some quick, non-fancy math on this situation. Let's say that no new business comes in, so the arrival rate is zero. The current team of six attorneys would have eight cases each. With a turnaround time of two weeks per case, each lawyer would have sixteen weeks to theoretically complete his or her work. That's almost a third of a year!

This means that if cases were handled sequentially or one at a time, our group had a lead process time of 112 days (sixteen weeks x seven—if you meet a lawyer who tells you that he or she doesn't work weekends they are probably lying!) for one attorney to handle a current level of cases effectively, which doesn't take into account the new business coming in.

So what should they do? Stop selling? Not likely.

The answer was, well, sort of. Our recommendation—at least the one they accepted—was to take a two-week break in selling to realign, regroup, and reassess the approach to delivering on their significant backlog. We used our Kanban method (the one that we described way back in Chapter Two) to break up the case load and establish an approach for incremental improvement. The great thing about Kanban is that it is a visual system that triggers an action. Kanban puts continuous improvement as a focus, manages the flow of work, and focuses the team on limiting the work in process. It was perfect for addressing this firm's issues, and we elected to pilot it for three months to see how the attorneys adopted it.

Step one was to reduce the size of the batches of work the attorneys in this practice group were discussing on a daily basis. Estate plans come in a number of shapes and sizes, so you can imagine the angst that all of them felt when they saw a large queue of work with some big, complex plans hidden inside getting larger by the day due to a hypercompetitive and hyperproductive sales team. The euphoria that a small business can feel from a healthy sales pipeline can turn to despair the minute the team responsible for doing or delivering the work feels that they will never catch up. Our charge for these folks was to stop, take a breath, and become Agile Thinkers. After all, if there ever was a group that needed some Agile Thinking, it was definitely these people!

One of the greatest changes in the Agile movement was how teams planned to deliver their work. According to one of the primary certification bodies of Agile practitioners and a recognized authority on the subject, a team's work, if digested correctly, can:

*deliver small batches of functionality that stakeholders can see and **inspect** at the end of every Sprint [iteration]. Then, based on that feedback, the Team can **adapt** their plans for the next batch of functionality. By learning early what works and what doesn't and whether an increment matches stakeholder expectations, the Team is ultimately able to deliver a full product that both satisfies and also delights customers.*[20]

So pairing smaller batch sizes for the team to digest with our tried-and-true Kanban system of managing workflow, we hypothesized that the two weeks spent planning and organizing the queue of work items would be well-served.

---

20 Scrum Alliance, Inc. "How Do Sprints and Increments Allow Scrum Teams to Inspect and Adapt?" Scrum Framework, accessed July 21, 2020.

The team struggled initially, as all teams do with new processes or methodologies, but over time began to see a stack of estate plans not as large blocks of work but a series of smaller, interconnected pieces of contract work that they could divide, review, and complete in a dynamic fashion. The team of lawyers learned that their own capacity, once defined as their collective ability to create and deliver entire estate plans from start to finish, became easier to manage once they were able to break up their estate plans into component parts. For context, your basic, run-of-the-mill estate plan typically has wills, a trust, a few different types of powers of attorney, and then maybe some related property transfer documents, like a deed. The group knew that some in their ranks were great at trusts, some better at wills, some awesome at property transfers. The team determined that if they formed three "pods" of lawyers—or, small teams with expertise in the parts of a client's estate that used to constrain them—they could turn around work much faster. Each new estate plan earned a spot on the Kanban board, and the new team pods built real discipline into selecting cases that suited their strengths. They ultimately got to the point where they knew how much each pod could achieve or complete in a single day, and their Agile Thinking journey was off and running!

Every day the team members would hold each other accountable by detailing what they did the prior day, what they would work on that day, and on any obstacles that stood in their path. Over the two-week period, the flow of work began to normalize and their backlog got a bit smaller. The team pushed itself to achieve or complete more in the span of each week and finally got to the point where their backlog of work was able to accommodate new sold business with little or no difficulty or consternation.

This is an example of how a normal, everyday group of people used Agile principles to become Agile Thinkers. Taking a step back from your daily grind and the other pressures that life puts upon us to view our work in smaller, more manageable chunks and then arranging those chunks in such a way that can move easily through lists of To-Do items, in-process items, and on to completed items can make the complex less so, the mundane more fun, and the stakeholders way more satisfied and engaged than they were before.

They also achieved something that many new Agile teams in software development endeavor do: they self-actualized. A self-actualizing team is a team dynamic where the team self-selects and self-manages the work that it is chartered to do. The team—and not some project manager, authority figure, or overlord—chooses the work that it intends to do, with a keen focus on what brings the most value to the organization. It's a big deal, folks. It's Agile Thinking nirvana!

The story doesn't end here. The team went so far as to arrange demonstrations back to the partner group every two weeks and began conducting regular "retrospective" meetings where the team would identify what worked well over the course of the last two weeks, what didn't work well, and what items, if any, they would choose to focus their collective energy to improve.

At the time of writing, this team has a perfect balance between the work coming in to the practice and the capacity of the team to deliver it. In most cases, their turnaround time for new legal business now exceeds the prior service agreement of two weeks. Client satisfaction improved, employee engagement became stronger, and efficiency skyrocketed. They are now one of the most consistently profitable and efficient firms in the area, all because they chose to view delivery through another lens.

In life, we all have leaps to take, and these lawyers are glad that they took one here.

CHAPTER TEN

HERDING CATS: USING AGILE TO APPLY TO COLLEGE

———

I love my first-born son dearly. Watching my wife give birth to him was the most amazing nineteen hours that I think I have spent on this planet, and it will forever be one moment that I will never forget for as long as I live. I love all of my kids, and think that the very process of childbirth—the fact that we can actually produce other humans within our own bodies—is a miracle unto itself, so at the grave risk of ignoring them and focusing on my oldest, I will tell you a story of how I am using our Agile principles to prepare him for the next chapter of his life.

College. Yeesh.

It's one of those future realities that all young parents think about but can't conceptualize. Look at them: all those young parents looking starry-eyed and hopeful toward that one shining moment when their son or daughter accepts that diploma from Stanford or Princeton then goes off to do amazing things like stabilize the climate or cure cancer. Given what we as humans have achieved over time, the possibilities for our little ones are absolutely limitless.

Those possibilities tend to narrow over time, which was definitely the case with my son, Sam. Sam is a great kid—he is mostly responsible, extraordinarily personable, and can go several layers deep into sports statistics, especially for his two passions in sports, the Chicago Blackhawks and the Green Bay Packers (we live in Chicago, where liking the latter can be listed legally as an "irreconcilable difference" in a divorce proceeding, but since he is not yet eighteen we are legally obligated to put up with it). Sam excels in dealing with people. He can talk to anyone, endear himself to any adult, and pretty much do what he wants with his interpersonal skills. These are definitely his strengths, which we believe will ultimately outweigh his primary limitation: his schoolwork.

Sam, God love him, is not a student. Like, not even a little bit. And he knows this too, as evidenced by the night that I was attempting to teach him basic multiplication in grade school. Nothing was sticking—nothing. Nada. Zeeeeerooooo. At one point, I looked up at him, exasperated, and said, "Sam, for the love of all that is good and holy, why can't you get these basic facts?"

His reply: "Dad, I got nothing for you here. It's not that I'm not trying; I just can't get my head around these numbers the way that you need me to."

A few moments later when I wiped those hot, guilty tears away, he totally trashed the moment with, "Besides, I put the 'stud' in student."

Fast forward through several "studdly" student years to his senior year of high school, where the two of us are not looking at multiplication tables anymore, but rather at the precipice of the deep abyss that is the college admissions process. Based on what you know of Sam so far, you can imagine how much work he has put into his college applications to this point and how much he understands what is asked of him by the schools to which he would like to apply. Hint: the answer does not include phrases like "clarity," or "laser-guided, pinpoint accuracy." Rather, he is lost. He is looking to me—his dad—for guidance and coaching, and is hopeful that I will give him a parachute that will actually open should he decide to take the plunge over that precipice and find himself *in extremis.*

The fact of the matter is that, well, I got nothing for you here, Sam. It's not that I'm not trying; I just can't get my head around guiding a teenager through a college admissions process because *I have never freaking done it before.* I applied to college in the early nineties, and we all know that things were night-and-day different then (fun fact: the year I applied to college I sent my first email ever to ask someone to prom, and then promptly decided that the concept would never take off). So why do you think that I am going to be of any value to you in the admissions process?

The answer, my good friends, lies within the very Agile Manifesto that we learned about in our earlier chapters.[21] The Manifesto, and all principles that form the foundation of the movement, can be an asset to Sam and me here, if only we were able to break them down into bite-sized pieces. Let's take a look. Based on what we know so far, we can think of this seemingly complex process as a project that can be accomplished by the following:

Using individuals and interactions over processes and tools: Daily check-ins with Sam include discussions around what he did yesterday in support of the application process, what he is doing today to further the application process, and what obstacles, if any, his coach and guide (i.e. me) can remove so that he can be successful. This is an exercise in accountability that can be applied to almost any situation, in any industry, or in any part of your personal lives. Holding people accountable is something that we should all do, all of the time.

Using the goal of a working end product (not necessarily software) over comprehensive documentation: Transcripts, essays, forms to fill out! Oh, my! For anyone who has gone through this process themselves or is doing what I am currently doing with Sam, you will definitely relate. This can be a lot, especially if you have an obligation to turn in multiple applications for your child or for yourself. The goal here is to focus on what "success" looks like—in this case, a completed college application—and begin to frame the tasks that will get you or yours to the point of success. By starting at the

---

21   "The Agile Manifesto," Agile Alliance, accessed July 20, 2020.

smallest level—the task—you can begin to sequence every piece of that application to the point where you are ready to send it in. Hooray!

Leveraging customer collaboration over contract negotiation: This one is a bit strange, especially if you aren't able to view the college as your customer or having issues with the whole negotiation piece. For Sam's application process, the college is his customer, "stud/student" remarks notwithstanding. At the end of the day, I believe that any college would be lucky to have Sam, provided he holds up his end of the bargain by applying himself and studying. My belief is that it isn't necessarily a transcript or an essay that sells a person into a college, but the person him or herself. Let your child determine the best way in which to engage with the (hopefully) accepting university and determine how he or she can let it hear his or her voice.

Sam's answer lies in the interview. We'll make sure that all of the i's are dotted and the t's are crossed on his application before we send him in there for his interview, which should seal the deal. We can revisit this one as we go.

Responding to change over following a plan: Not only is this one of the most versatile parts of the manifesto to apply to our daily lives, it is one of the best life lessons to teach a young adult. How many times did we as late teenagers or our kids as late teenagers think that the only acceptable answer when encountering a perceived failure or large roadblock was to quit? Betting dollars to doughnuts that the answer is "lots" here is a sucker bet. Dealing with roadblocks or failures is something that all of us—including and especially our children—need to learn how to handle. Being nimble, or dare I say agile, in all things allows us to be able to see problems from different angles and gives us an opportunity to solve them in a way that best suits our brains or levels of ability.

Let's take a look at how Sam worked with my wife and me to get to the point where any obstacle—no matter how big or how small—was not an issue but an opportunity for him to solve and get stronger.

The applications process typically follows these general steps, which are in no particular order:

1. Find an application;
2. Fill out said application;
3. Complete and revise any admissions essay(s);
4. Get copies of your high school transcripts;
5. Pay some sort of fee; and
6. Compile and mail the application to your school of choice.

While this greatly oversimplified list may seem pretty straightforward to most people, to my son this may as well be the assembly instructions for *The Titanic*. To him, this list, and all subtasks that lie behind each item, is a batch of complexity that he either can't or won't tackle. He doesn't need someone like yours truly to apply for him, as that isn't what he wants; rather, he needs to be coached on how to think about the problem differently, and our working hypothesis with him was that we could use Agile to do it.

Using our interpersonal interaction, I made sure that the first lesson that young Sam learned here was one of accountability.

Interpersonal interactions to a professional like a software developer means that the person not only has access to other resources in a self-actualizing team, but also that person has a daily status meeting where s/he has to report on what s/he did yesterday, what s/he is doing today, and what obstacles, if any, stand in the way of success. For a number of years, I jokingly called this "management by passive aggression," because the more times someone gives the same update with no progress, the more the team rides that person. It's a wonderful way to get the most out of your people—you would be surprised at what group dynamics occur when they put themselves on report.

So every day Sam and I would meet for ten to fifteen minutes to discuss his overall progress on the work that he had to do to complete the application. What he did yesterday fed directly in what he was supposed to do that day, and any identified obstacles discussed gave me the opportunity to provide coaching, which is something that made him feel better about this rather intimidating process.

Never underestimate the power of comfort. Once you put someone at ease with the concepts around completing a really hard task, you will have a devoted resource, employee, friend, or as we see here, a family member at your disposal.

Once we started to meet on a daily basis, we needed to find a way to track our progress. Because we as humans need to believe that we can't manage what we don't measure, we needed a way to ensure that progress was being made and that we were heading in a direction that got young Sam where he needed to go. There are a number of applications and methods you can use to track project progress, so in this case we went with good old Trello, as we believed that Kanban would support our needs. We organized our Trello board to accommodate tasks for our backlog, a clean "WIP" column so that we can manage our in-process work, and created a "Complete" column so that we can feel like we made real progress. Because breaking down tasks into these three categories was something that we could all get our heads around, we chose it. Now we needed some easy-to-use tasks to get into Trello so that we could get Sam moving.

After taking a day to revel in our success in selecting a tool (yay, us!) we started to take the six items in the application list above and break them down into pieces that could be easily actioned and completed. Now, remember: software developers using Agile utilize something called "user stories" to describe the often-complex requirements that they have to take from a non-technical business person and turn them into working, technically efficient pieces of production-ready software code. We, as Agile Thinkers, can definitely do the same.

A user story follows a simple format: "As a [type of end user] I want to [be able to do something, like click a button or calculate a number] so that [I can get the output or end result that I want]. We won't dwell on user stories here, but the concept is pretty universal. Essentially, the goal of any Agile Thinker is to break down tasks—no matter how large or how small—into basic units of work that can be delivered in a short amount of time. This is what I did with Sam on this process. Taking the first items on the list (finding and filling out the application for his chosen school), we determined together what success looks like at the end of a two week period, and then we worked backward to what he would need to do on the daily to get us to where we need to go. For example, day one's story was to find the application. Easy win. Sam rolled in to our second status meeting with a smile on his face and a completed task. Bam.

From that point on, things got a bit harder. Not much, but just enough to keep us challenged and keep the discussion flowing in our daily meetings. The application was organized into sections—as most applications are—so we were able to take a section or two at a time until list items one and two were completed. There were days when he was able to complete a portion and state what section he was going to handle next, and there were days when I could tell that he wasn't making any measurable progress at all. Every day, I had opportunities to either coach or praise him, which feels good as a parent.

I'll forever remember our "status meetings" fondly as time well spent. Some dads play catch with their kids; others, like me, hold status meetings. Amazing.

And, in case you're wondering, he got in. It was a great day for "studs" and Agile Thinkers alike!

CHAPTER ELEVEN

WHY AND HOW I WROTE THIS BOOK AS AN AGILE THINKER

———

Every single moment of taking this book from concept to finished product was a paradigm of perfect Agile efficiency. I'm an expert, after all.

Can you hear that sound? Yep, that's the sound of my publisher and marketing and revisions editor laughing hysterically. During the course of our efforts to get this book to print, I'm pretty sure there were multiple instances when my marketing editor actually wanted to run me over with her car. Here I was, preaching efficiency and effectiveness while I was, at times, neither efficient nor effective.

When I finally decided to take the leap and put my opinions about this subject on paper, I knew that I couldn't write a ton about Agile, as there are already entire cottage industries centered around things like Agile coaching, backlog management, product development, and using Agile at scale. My intent was to key in on a few Agile and continuous improvement concepts to enable anyone with a busy life to live, work, and manage more efficiently. This was going to be my attempt to bring Silicon Valley to Main Street, USA, but it quickly became a surprisingly formidable task. Apparently, it's not easy to write a book while helping to run a six-person household and leading a large, distributed organization from the comfort (or, more accurately, chaos) of my own home because of a pandemic and civil unrest. On top of it all, my Wi-Fi router had to simultaneously support near-constant WebExes, eLearning sessions via Zoom, Netflix streaming, and a Call of Duty playing teenager. I nearly wrote an apology letter to my router in the form of an afterword to this book. The struggle was real.

Like many other people dealing with 2020, there were times I felt overwhelmed and exhausted by it all. To be completely honest, I reached the point of feeling like we were one massive asteroid strike away from making this year *really* complete. Bring it on, universe. Bring it on.

But you know what? That's life, folks. Being human is never easy, because stuff just keeps getting in the way. The minute you feel that you have your affairs in order, you encounter anywhere from one to seventeen obstacles that spring up in your way. This is just how life unfolds, and sometimes it's all we can do just to make our way through it.

This book was no different. I never intended for this book to answer the meaning of life, nor did I necessarily want it shelved next to *Anna Karenina*. I wanted to present you with some lessons I learned along my professional journey that ultimately became *super* hard to complete. In reality, creating *The Agile Thinker* was precisely the type of project that I wanted to write about. Just as I got into writing the substantive content of this book—and believe me, I used a Trello board, personal backlog, utilized stories, the whole nine yards—I experienced the same challenges that the rest of us face when running our households, keeping our jobs, and just generally maintaining our state of affairs as people.

So when deadlines were tight and expectations were high, I took a breath and focused on one or two tools that brought this book to the point where you, dear reader, can consume it. I actually walked across that bridge that I built—piece by piece—on my own Agile Thinking journey and used it to do my best to figure out how to take my book the rest of the way.

If there is one lesson or takeaway that I want you absorb by reading this, it's exactly that: find a few techniques in this book that work for you and let those techniques be a bridge that helps you more effectively deal with life's complexities. Use a Trello or a Kanban board at home to organize a big project, just like my friend with his basement. Figure out how much work you can get done in a day and start measuring your velocity. Utilize WIP to determine how your work flows from your stakeholders to your To-Do list and off your plate, like my law firm client. Whatever works for you! If you can successfully bring this to fruition, then you have built your own bridge. All you need to do now is to figure out how to take those techniques and make them work for you and your life. Once your Trello board is in place, determine how to work on the most important items first, or to not only *measure* your velocity but learn how to *improve* your velocity to become *faster* at getting things done. Impress your boss with a discussion on WIP and how you, like Disney, make sure that you can complete your work list items efficiently enough to keep everyone happy (or most everyone, if we're being real). This book is intended to get you halfway there, and by becoming an Agile Thinker, you will have the tools to determine *your* best way of taking those last few steps.

You can do this!

I hope that as you read through this book you were able to connect to one (or several) of the techniques, tips, tricks, and hacks that we learned together in *The Agile Thinker*. I welcome and would love to hear any ideas or success stories that you personally experienced as a result. Feedback is a gift, after all, so don't be shy.

I hope you are successful in becoming more efficient and effective, but most of all, I hope you always move ever forward.

Welcome to the team, Agile Thinker. Now let's get to work.

ACKNOWLEDGEMENTS

———

Well, this book can't be all theory, right?

Consider this book to be a basic toolbox for your Agile Thinking journey.

The techniques in this book, as well as the stories I related from my professional past, are merely items that I have used along my Agile Thinking path, and I hope that they will serve you well as you go through yours.

And the best part? These tools don't require any storage space in your garage! My gift to you.

None of this would have been possible without the guidance, mentorship, and examples set by a number of different people. As with any movement, those who try, who do, and who may succeed only do so by standing on the shoulders of others before them.

For starters, I'd like to take a minute to tip my cap to those intrepid souls who created the Agile framework only because they decided to self-actualize and talk about a better way of working. The signers of the Manifesto changed business that day, and they changed the lives of many folks just like me.

I'd like to thank Mr. Mike Beedle, one of those signers of the Manifesto, for training me in the dark arts of Agile. Unfortunately, Mike is no longer with us, but his example and guidance will remain with me forever.

I would like to thank my wife of twenty-one (but who's counting?) years, Heather. Heather is my life partner, my best friend, and also my attorney. Thank you for keeping me sane, keeping me focused on this project, and keeping me out of jail, honey. You rock.

I would like to thank the coaches, the consultants, and the clients who allowed me to grow along the way, and I wish them the very best in their lives and careers going forward.

Professor Eric Koester and the good folks at New Degree Press gave me a shot to write and release this book, and for that I am ever grateful.

I also want to thank you—the reader—for taking the time to read this. I hope that you start an Agile Thinking movement of your own, and that your life is somehow better because of it.

Since feedback is a gift, I would love to hear what worked well for you, what didn't work so well, and any items that you feel should deserve more of a focus for you and other Agile Thinkers along the way.

APPENDIX

INTRODUCTION TO THE INTRODUCTION

Hohlbaum, Christine Louise. "How Can We Keep up in This Fast-Paced World?" *The Power of Slow* (blog). *Psychology Today*, November 14, 2009. https://www.psychologytoday.com/us/blog/the-power-slow/200911/how-can-we-keep-in-fast-paced-world

CHAPTER ONE: THE SCIENCE BEHIND THE AGILE THINKER

Agile Alliance. "Manifesto for Agile Software Development." Accessed August 19, 2020. http://agilemanifesto.org/.

Mike Tyson's famous "Everyone has a plan until they get punched in the mouth" quote was in response to a question from a sports reporter that asked if he was worried about Evander Holyfield's fight plan.

Royce, Winston W. "Managing the Development of Large Software Systems." Paper presented at the meeting of the Proceedings IEEE WESCON, 1970.

CHAPTER TWO: MAKING LIFE EASIER BY MASTERING YOUR WIP

Little, J. D. C. "A Proof for the Queuing Formula: $L = \lambda W$." *Operations Research*. 9, no. 3 (1961): 383–387.

Ōno, Taiichi. *Toyota Production System: Beyond Large-Scale Production*. Cambridge, Mass: Productivity Press, 1988.

RCI Consulting. "Little's Law at Disney." November 23, 2013. Video, 1:56. https://www.youtube.com/watch?v=nl7hARdw18M.

Scaled Agile, Inc. "Principle #6—Visualize and Limit WIP, Reduce Batch Sizes, and Manage Queue Lengths." Accessed July 21, 2020. https://www.scaledagileframework.com/visualize-and-limit-wip-reduce-batch-sizes-and-manage-queue-lengths/.

SECTION TWO: THE FOUNDATIONS

This quote was made famous by the comedian Steve Martin. The full text reads, "Before you criticize a man, walk a mile in his shoes. That way, when you do criticize him, you'll be a mile away and have his shoes."

CHAPTER THREE: MAKING THE LEAP: BECOMING AN AGILE THINKER

Greengrass, Paul, Billy Ray, Scott Rudin, Dana Brunetti, Michael De Luca, Gregory Goodman, Eli Bush. *Captain Phillips*. Culver City, CA: Sony Pictures Home Entertainment (Firm). 2014

Haber, George. "The Impact of the Subconscious on Risk-Based Decision Making." *EHS Today*. Accessed July 21, 2020. https://

www.ehstoday.com/safety-leadership/article/21917852/the-impact-of-the-subconscious-on-riskbased-decision-making.

Scrum Alliance, Inc. "Overview: What Is Scrum?" Accessed July 21, 2020. https://www.scrumalliance.org/about-scrum/overview.

CHAPTER FOUR: GETTING ALIGNED

Murphy, Karen, Christopher Guest, Michael McKean, Harry Shearer, and Rob Reiner. *This is Spinal Tap*. Santa Monica, CA: Metro Goldwyn Mayer Home Entertainment. 1984.

CHAPTER FIVE: WHAT'S YOUR STORY?

Wake, Bill. "INVEST in Good Stories, and SMART Tasks," *XP123: Exploring Extreme Programming* (blog), August 17, 2003. https://xp123.com/articles/invest-in-good-stories-and-smart-tasks/.

CHAPTER SIX: MASTERING SPACE AND TIME USING BACKLOGS

Rubin, Kenneth S. *Essential Scrum: A Practical Guide to the Most Popular Agile Process.* Upper Saddle River, NJ: Pearson Education, Inc, 2012.

Scrum Alliance, Inc. "Overview: What Is Scrum?" Accessed July 21, 2020. https://www.scrumalliance.org/about-scrum/overview.

CHAPTER SEVEN: OUR NEW NORMAL: MANAGING BACKLOGS AMIDST A PANDEMIC, AND OTHER CHEERFUL TOPICS

Holtz, Lou. *Winning Every Day: The Game Plan for Success.* New York: Harper Business, 1998.

World Health Organization. "Plague Fact Sheet." Last modified October 2017. http://who.int/news-room/fact-sheets/detail/plague.

CHAPTER EIGHT: CONNECTING THE DOTS: MANAGING YOUR FLOW AS AN AGILE THINKER

Lean Enterprise Institute, Inc. "Knowledge Center: Flow," Lean Institute Knowledge Center. Accessed July 21, 2020. https://www.lean.org/search/?sc=flow.

SECTION THREE: THE STORIES
LAWYERS CAN BE AGILISTS TOO!

Chelst, Kenneth, and Edwards, Tom. "Queuing Systems and Formula," High School Operations Research (HSOR). Accessed July 21, 2020. http://www.hsor.org/what_is_or.cfm?name=queuing_systems_formula.

Masicampo, E. J., and Baumeister, R. F. "Consider It Done! Plan Making Can Eliminate the Cognitive Effects of Unfulfilled Goals." *Journal of Personality and Social Psychology* 101, (June 2011): 667-683.

Scrum Alliance, Inc. "How Do Sprints and Increments Allow Scrum Teams to Inspect and Adapt?" Scrum Framework. Accessed July 21, 2020. https://www.scrumalliance.org/about-scrum/framework.

HERDING CATS: USING AGILE TO APPLY TO COLLEGE

Agile Alliance. "Manifesto for Agile Software Development." Accessed August 19, 2020. http://agilemanifesto.org/.

Made in the USA
Monee, IL
22 August 2022

12183710R10085